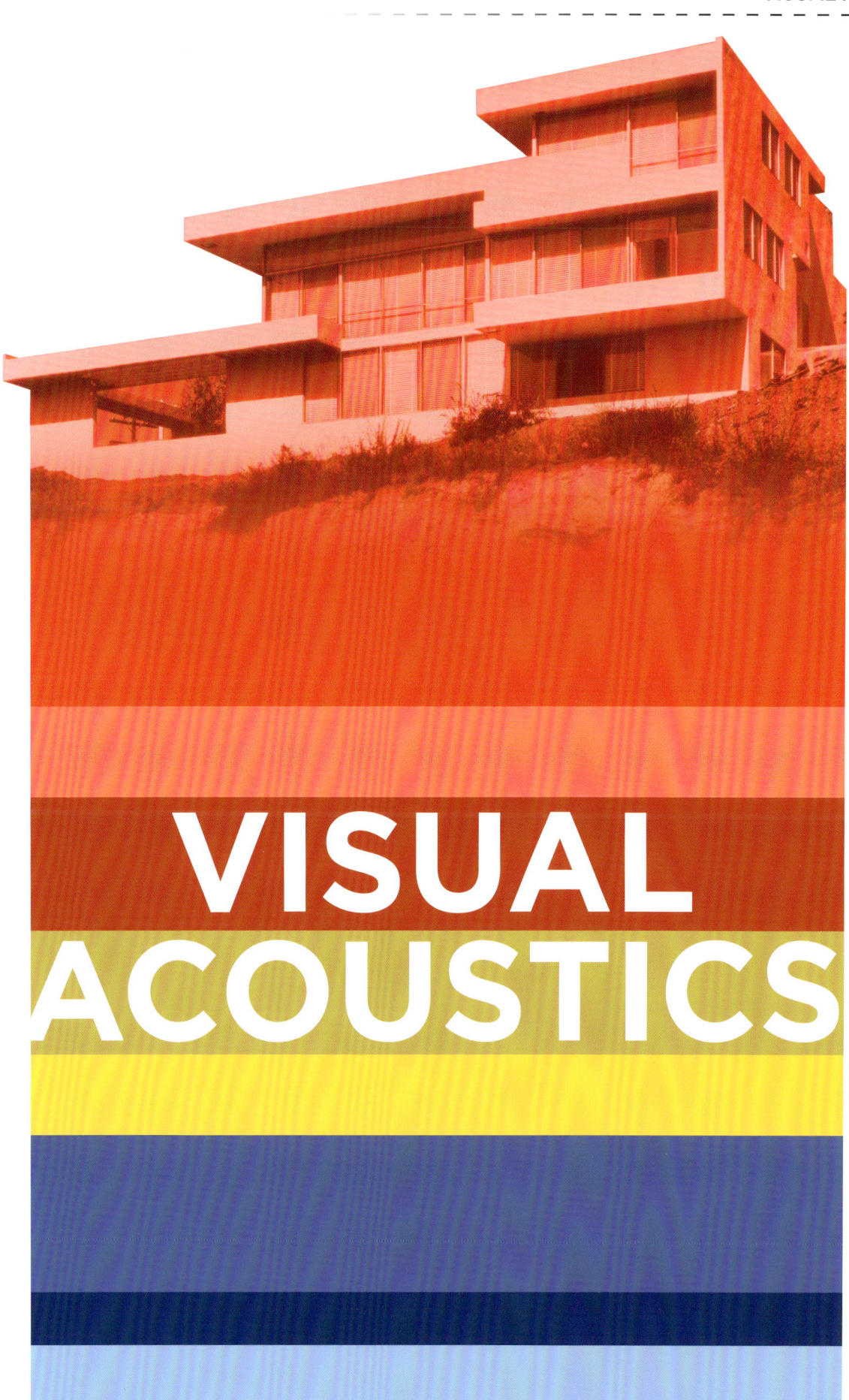

ABOUT THE AUTHOR:
WILL PAICE

Will Paice is an author, filmmaker, digital marketer, designer and architecture enthusiast. After 20 years in the film and television industries in London and Los Angeles, Will now lives and works in Kent with his wife and children.

In 1997, Will moved from London to Hollywood, California to work at Panavision, the iconic film services company. It was during this time that he developed his passion for the newly rediscovered midcentury architecture of southern California, and became involved in the preservation and restoration of landmark properties in LA and Palm Springs.

In 2003, he met Julius Shulman by the pool at Orbit In, a "motor court inn" designed by Herb Burns and completed in 1957. Nestled under the dramatic San Jacinto Mountains in the historic Tennis Club District (a hangout for Hollywood stars since the 1930s) the hotel provided a dramatic setting for a conversation with the maestro of midcentury architectural photography, who would go on to become the subject for the documentary, *Visual Acoustics: The Modernism of Julius Shulman.*

VISUAL ACOUSTICS

THE MODERNISM OF JULIUS SHULMAN

WILL PAICE

ACKNOWLEDGEMENTS

Albert Hill and Matt Gibberd from The Modern House for being so helpful with the early UK screenings of **Visual Acoustics** as well as for helping to arrange the filming of the "Paice on Shulman" interview at the Rogers House in Wimbledon, UK.

Ab Rogers and Philippa Wyatt for generously allowing us to film the "Paice on Shulman" interview at the Rogers House in Wimbledon, UK.

My wife, Charlotte Wontner, for being so tirelessly supportive and patient over the many years that this project took to come to fruition.

Allan Temko (1924–2006), Pulitzer Prize-winning former *San Francisco Chronicle* architecture critic, who kindled my interest in modern art, architecture and activism and provided great inspiration over the 40 years that we knew each other.

Andrea Fiuczynski (with whom I met Julius Shulman for the first time by the pool at Orbit In) for introducing me to Palm Springs and so much more.

Vicky Jung, script editor extraordinaire, whose notes on the first draft of this book were invaluable.

James Middleton for his patience and diligence while editing the book.

Everyone credited in the film, without whose invaluable help and advice it would never have been made.

All the wonderful, innovative, daring, creative architects of the midcentury period whose courage and energy helped to forge a new world in the west.

...and of course, Julius Shulman, for being the maestro.

First edition published in 2019 by Network Distributing Ltd.

Will Paice in association with Hopscotch Studios Ltd. presented by Network Distributing Ltd.

7958101 • ISBN 978-0-9929766-5-1

Typeset and designed by Network Distributing.
Creative direction/Project manager - Omar McAlpine
Designer - Rob White
Executive Producer - Tim Beddows

Printed and bound by Healeys Printers Ltd.

CONTENTS

FOREWORD BY ERIC BRICKER

Visual Acoustics: The Modernism Of Julius Shulman premiered at the Los Angeles Film Festival (LAFF) on June 22, 2008. Julius attended every sold-out screening; each had an audience filled with family, friends, and representatives from the architecture and design world. In addition to being the ideal venue at which to unveil this Los Angeles story, LAFF also proved the most fitting festival for us to secure our distributor, Arthouse Films. Specialising in art and architecture related content, Arthouse opened the film theatrically on October 9, 2009, at Cinema Village in New York. The film screened in theatres across the US through March of 2010. To this day, *Visual Acoustics* continues to play to audiences worldwide. The release of this special Blu-ray edition by Network Distributing Limited, ten years after its festival premiere, affirms that interest in Julius, his photography, and the work of so many great modern architects continues to broaden.

From the beginning, this film was a labour of love for all of those who said "yes" to participate in its creation. One of the principal contributors was entrepreneur, photographer, and former president of Panavision, Will Paice. Julius introduced me to Will in 2004, shortly after they had spent a Palm Springs poolside afternoon together at the Orbit In. Will's interest in all things photography, architecture, and California ultimately led him to serve as our co-producer. His input and support were vital in achieving our project's ambitious outcome. Ten years later, Will has once again so graciously contributed his time, expertise, and artful eye, this time in the form of writing the accompanying book you now hold in your hands. I find his impeccable scholarship and unwavering passion emblematic of who he is as a person. In addition to Will serving as a tireless champion of this film, he has also become a dear friend to me.

In May of 2012, Will and his partner, Charlotte Wontner of Hopscotch Films, screened *Visual Acoustics* for press and potential UK distributors at The Soho Hotel's screening room in London. Amongst the audience was Network Distributing's Managing Director, Tim Beddows. In an email to Will the day after the screening, Tim wrote, "I saw the film with two colleagues and we all felt the same way about it: uplifting, inspiring, very informative, and beautifully made." Tim agreed to distribute the film in the UK and this Blu-ray package is one of the fruits of that agreement. Tim's unique and engaging approach to distributing content is truly a gift to me as a filmmaker. Tim, on behalf of all who were involved in the making of this film, thank you for your belief in and commitment to *Visual Acoustics*.

In October 2012, I met Omar McAlpine at a London screening of *Visual Acoustics* at the Royal Institute of British Architects. His enthusiasm for the film and its subject matter was evident upon our first meeting; it has not waned since. Omar has served as the creative director of this Blu-ray edition. Without his persistence of vision and attention to detail we would not have been able to produce what is, to me, the ultimate package I had always envisioned. I know Julius is looking down from his studio in the sky and smiling upon Omar's work. Omar is a true ally of this film, and he, too, has become a dear friend.

Julius was one of the great photographers, not only of the 20th Century, but also of the photographic medium itself. His 1960 photograph of the Stahl House (Case Study House #22) is considered by *TIME Magazine* to be one of the 100 most influential photographs of all time. Often while visiting Julius I would observe a fresh batch of international periodicals featuring his photographs strewn across the work surfaces in his studio. He would point to a pile, smile and say, "It [the fascination] never ends." His name and body of work continue to gain wider global recognition as the Shulman Archive, permanently housed at the Getty Research Institute, is now accessible online to everyone in the world.

Although Julius passed away in July of 2009, his spirit is alive and well. Julius captured, communicated, and promoted a zeitgeist while simultaneously encouraging others to express their own interpretation of it. It was more than architecture and photography for him. It was about pursuing one's deepest longings and desires, for he was both a master photographer and a master of living life.

In closing, I truly hope that you enjoy this Blu-ray package and feel inspired by its content. It has been a privilege to work with this material again and have a final product that I feel so happy to present. Equally, your interest, time, and passion for this subject matter and film are appreciated beyond measure.

Eric Bricker
Austin, Texas, United States
June 2018

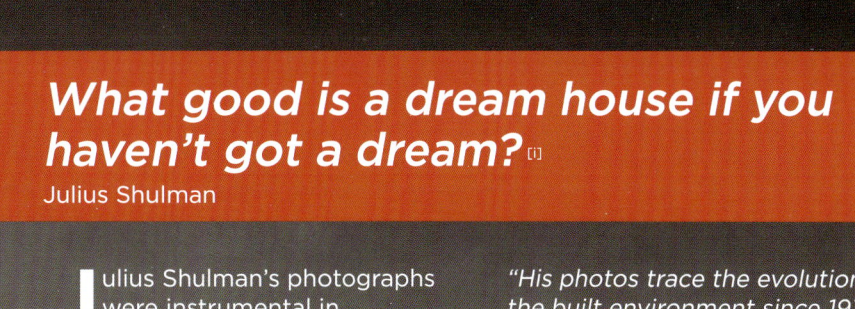

What good is a dream house if you haven't got a dream? [i]
Julius Shulman

Julius Shulman's photographs were instrumental in implanting midcentury modern architecture into the consciousness of the twentieth century and beyond. His images depict the architects' intent, the temporal and spatial relevance of the structures, and the spirit of the people who inhabited them. They capture the energy and optimism of post-World War II southern California in a style of architecture and design devoted to the romance of the machine and the quest for a new way of living.

Shulman's images continue to be of crucial importance to historians and twentieth century cultural history:

"His photos trace the evolution of the built environment since 1936, giving insight into construction techniques, urban development, real estate, the advent of tourism in the jet age, and, of course, the history of Los Angeles." [ii]

Shulman helped to break down the barriers between photography and art, his images transcending the primary intent for which they were commissioned. His clarity, innovation, intuitive sense of composition, and timing have earned Shulman a reputation as the greatest architectural photographer of the twentieth century and one of the pre-eminent artists of the West Coast.

SHULMAN THE ICON MAKER

The year is 1960. Elvis Presley returns from two years of military service in Germany and records *Are You Lonesome Tonight?* The Cold War is at its height and the situation in Vietnam is escalating. In December, John F. Kennedy will replace Dwight Eisenhower as president of the United States (US), marking a radical change in post-war politics.

Some 2,300 miles (3,700 kilometres) west of the White House, where southern California tumbles into the Pacific Ocean, the streetlights of the City of Angels converge as they extend south towards a vanishing point near LAX airport. The Santa Anas bring a warm desert breeze from the east, clearing the smog that normally obscures the city. Perched nearly 200 feet (60 metres) above Sunset Boulevard in the Hollywood Hills, a new and elegantly simple house emerges from a precarious platform.

A photographer with a gift for being in the right place at the right time steadies his tripod in the hot tub beside the house. He arranges the edges of the overhanging roof in his viewfinder to mirror the lines of the streets below in a symphony of horizontal and converging diagonal lines. He checks the composition: two girls in cocktail dresses chatting about the evening ahead framed behind the plate glass windows of the house. He squeezes the shutter release, triggering strobe lights that illuminate the interior. The shutter stays open for seven minutes to expose the city lights. An icon is born.

The house is the Stahl House, the photographer is Julius Shulman: the resulting image has become perhaps the most evocative symbol of the relaxed, modern lifestyle associated with post-war Los Angeles and West Coast living. It was, as architecture critic Paul Goldberger wrote in *The New York Times*, "one of those singular images that sum up an entire city at a moment in time."[iii] It went on to win first prize in the American Institute of Architects (AIA) National Award Competition for Architectural Photography and has been published innumerable times around the world. In November 2016, TIME magazine named the Stahl House photo one of the most influential in history.[iv]

"A dramatic photograph can have such a strong impact that it doesn't remain a simple reproduction of architecture but in fact an icon and symbol itself."[v] Perhaps no other image in the history of architectural photography better reflects this statement.

The house was the dream of ex-professional football player C.H. 'Buck' Stahl, and his wife Carlotta, who in 1954 bought the vacant lot for $13,500, the price of a three-bedroom house at the time. The ruggedly vertiginous site proved challenging to say the least. In 1959 the Stahls employed Pierre Koenig (1925–2004), an ambitious 32-year-old architect, to enable them to realise their vision of a light, L-shaped dwelling of steel and glass.

From here one of the quintessential works of twentieth century architecture was realised, projected onto the retina of the world by Shulman's abiding image. The architecture is remarkable enough. But Shulman's photograph, a 'constructed view' that transcends the simple structure seated precipitously on a cliff's edge, communicates directly with the observer. It reflects the viewer's dreams and desires, the prevailing economic and political climate, and the optimism of post-war US hegemony.

Julius Shulman photographing Case Study House #22 (Stahl House) Los Angeles, California. 1960

Case Study House #22 (Stahl House) Los Angeles, California. 1960
Architect: Pierre Koenig

SETTING THE SCENE:
MODERNISM COMES TO CALIFORNIA

During the nineteenth century, technological advances emerging from the Industrial Revolution had gradually come to be reflected in architecture. In the US, Chicago-based architect Louis Sullivan (1856–1924), "The Father of Skyscrapers"[vi] and even "The Father of Modernism",[vii] had coined the phrase "form ever follows function", condensed to 'form follows function', the battle cry of the new Modernists. Although attributed to him, Sullivan himself credited the idea to Marcus Vitruvius Pollio (born c. 80–70 BC, died after c. 15 BC), a Roman architect, engineer, and author of *De architectura*, who first argued that a structure must exhibit the three essential qualities of *firmitas, utilitas* and *venustas*: it must be solid, useful and beautiful.[viii]

This credo, which placed the demands of practical use above aesthetics, would later be adopted by architects of the Modernist movement to imply that decorative elements, or ornamentation, were superfluous in modern buildings. Sullivan argued that verticality was the perfect architectural expression of both modern construction techniques and the spirit of the new age. In contrast to Gothic, Classical, Romanesque or Renaissance architectural styles, the new architecture would be functional and reduce superfluous decoration. It would make use of new building materials such as steel, reinforced concrete and glass, rectilinear façades, cuboidal forms and height: all embodied in the skyscraper.

Having travelled extensively in the US from 1893 to 1896, Austrian architect Adolf Loos (1870–1933) was a devotee of Sullivan's architectural proclamations and helped to define Modernism in European architecture. Loos' seminal manifesto *Ornament and Crime*,[ix] denouncing the current vogue for Art Nouveau, proclaimed that *"The evolution of culture marches with the elimination of ornament from useful objects"*.

Lovell Health House
Los Angeles, California. 1950
Architect: Richard Neutra

Le Corbusier and colleagues

"A house is a machine for living in"[x]
Le Corbusier

Sullivan's influence on European architecture was further promoted when his former apprentice, Frank Lloyd Wright (1867–1959), left the US for Berlin in 1909. Wright's two-volume Wasmuth Folios was published in 1911[xi], profoundly influencing many thought leaders including Rudolph Schindler (1887–1953) and Richard Neutra (1892–1970), two young Austrian-born architecture students of Loos at the Vienna University of Technology.

The horrors of the First World War in Europe between 1914 and 1918 brought fundamental shifts in the traditional European class structure and mobility. The 'upstairs, downstairs' hierarchy was challenged in the trenches and led to a new social awareness of the inequalities that had defined pre-war society. Germany's defeat created political, economic and social upheaval that broke down the old imperial order

and forced architects to visualise a new, more formal and expressive style to rebuild the devastated country.

By the end of the First World War, it was argued that architecture had a moral obligation to reflect the spirit of the modern age. Modernism was a cultural response to these new conditions, and it was believed that it had the power to transform how people lived and worked. Functional design for mass production and distribution was seen as a means of repairing the devastating social damage the war had done.

In 1923, Swiss-born architect, designer, painter, writer and urban planner Le Corbusier (1887–1965, born Charles-Édouard Jeanneret-Gris) called on architects to reject the traditional and embrace the new values of the modern age through his published collection of essays, Vers Une Architecture.[xii]

His thesis in effect laid down the organising principles for the Modernist movement in architecture, advocating that efficient, industrialised architecture was the only way to avoid class-based upheaval, manifested in his maxim, "Architecture or Revolution." Le Corbusier united the functionalist aspirations of his generation with a strong grasp of the principles of expressionism. He was the first architect to use rough-cast concrete, a technique that expressed his asceticism and sympathy for sculptural forms.

In 1917, at the age of 30 and still known as Jeanneret-Gris, he returned to live in Paris, where he met the painter and designer Amédée Ozenfant, who introduced him to sophisticated contemporary art. Ozenfant initiated Jeanneret-Gris into Purism, his new pictorial aesthetic that rejected the complicated abstractions of Cubism and returned to the pure, simple geometric forms of everyday objects.

It was Ozenfant who suggested that Jeanneret changed his name to Le Corbusier (derived from le corbeau, french for 'raven'), the name of a paternal forebear.

Le Corbusier set about designing houses in France using modern industrial methods and materials. He developed a model for a "Machine for Living", embodied in his design for the Villa Savoye near Paris, France (completed 1931), one of the most famous houses of the European modern movement.

In Germany, Walter Gropius (1883–1969) and Ludwig Mies van der Rohe (1886–1969), were also developing a new architectural style. Gropius and van der Rohe had trained with Le Corbusier under Peter Behrens (1868–1940), one of the leaders of architectural reform at the turn of the century. Together, they were principals of the Bauhaus school, which Gropius had founded in Weimar, Germany, in 1919. Under their direction, the Bauhaus emerged as one of the most influential forces behind Modernist architecture, photography and design, and would have a profound impact on art, graphic design and typography, as well as architecture.

Consistent with the modern design advocated by Sullivan, the absence of ornamentation and harmony between form and function marked the Bauhaus model. It was governed by objective rationalism, economy, and modern technology and construction methods, together described as Neue Sachlichkeit (New Objectivity). In contrast to the sometimes rounded and abstracted forms of German Expressionist architecture of the 1910s and 1920s, New Objectivity was defined by rectilinear lines and planar surfaces, founded on a principle of rationality, to make the best use of industrial materials in an age of austerity.

In 1911, while at the Vienna Academy of Fine Arts, Schindler was introduced to Wright's architecture through his Wasmuth Folio. Having completed his thesis in 1913, Schindler moved to Chicago. He finally met his hero on 30 December 1914 and was hired to work on Wright's Imperial Hotel in Tokyo, before being summoned to Los Angeles in 1920 to oversee the building of the Hollyhock House in East Hollywood. The house was completed in 1921 while Wright was still in Japan.

Schindler had met Neutra at university in 1912. Graduating from the Vienna University of Technology in 1918, Neutra followed his friend to the US in 1923, where he worked briefly with Wright at the Taliesin Studio in Wisconsin before accepting Schindler's invitation to join him in California. The two set up in practice together, living with their wives in Schindler's experimental communal house and studio on King's Road, West Hollywood.

A decade later, Gropius and Mies van der Rohe moved to the US when the Nazi Party closed the Bauhaus school in 1933 for being 'un-German' in its Jewish-influenced 'cosmopolitan Modernism.' The year before, an exhibition at the Museum of Modern Art (MoMA) in New York entitled 'The International Style: Architecture Since 1922' had established Modernist architecture's place on the global stage. The exhibition and accompanying book,[xiii] compiled by US architect Philip Johnson (1906–2005) and architectural historian Henry-Russell

Lovell Beach House Newport Beach, California. 1968
Architect: Rudolph Schindler

Kaufmann Desert House Palm Springs, California. 1947
Architect: Richard Neutra

Hitchcock (1903–1987), identified three core themes: the expression of volume rather than mass, an emphasis on balance rather than preconceived symmetry, and the exclusion of applied ornament.

The show introduced Le Corbusier, Gropius and Mies van der Rohe to the American public, and also featured the architecture of Wright and Neutra. It brought European Modernist architecture to the attention of Americans and gave it a name: the International Style. Gropius eventually arrived at the Harvard Graduate School of Design in 1937 and Mies van der Rohe moved to Chicago in the same year to head the newly formed Illinois Institute of Technology (IIT). Here he designed the buildings and master plan for the campus.

Having collaborated with Schindler on several important commissions, including Philip Lovell's Beach House in Newport Beach (completed in 1926), Neutra went on to start his own practice, designing buildings in southern California that exemplified the International Style. Among his most recognised works were the Lovell Health House (1929), the Kaufmann Desert House (1946) and the VDL Research House (1966). His designs were celebrated for the rigorously geometric structure that embodied the midcentury modern aesthetic.

In the 1930s, Neutra's Los Angeles practice trained several young architects, including Gregory Ain (1908–1988), Harwell Hamilton Harris (1903–1990) and Raphael Soriano (1904–1988), all of whom went on to enjoy successful careers designing modern architecture in a West Coast variant of the International Style. Modernist architecture truly came into its own on an international stage after the Second World War, its broad social agenda directing much of the rebuilding programme after the war as soldiers returned home and bombed cities were rebuilt.

Below: Rudolph Schindler with Richard Neutra and family

SHULMAN'S EARLY YEARS

Julius Shulman was born in Brooklyn on 10 October 1910 – "10.10.10", as he liked to put it – the fourth of five children (Shirley, Lee, Ben, Julius and Sylvan). Shulman's parents, Max and Yetta, were Russian Jews, who had emigrated to the US as children with their parents. When Julius was just four months old Max and Yetta moved their young family from Brooklyn, where they had a candy store, to Connecticut. In 1914 they bought a 100-acre (40-hectare) farm in Central Village, Plainfield.

The enterprising Max, typical of the immigrant spirit, also set up business trading furs from northern New England and the Canadian New Brunswick province with furriers in New York.[xiv]

Shulman's memories of those days were acute: *"Many wild animals inhabited the forests. Deer, fox, raccoons, possum are some I recall. I remember one day my father chasing a deer trying to catch it for me, but it jumped over a fence, away it went."*[xv]

Julius would remember the first time he saw an automobile:

"One day we heard a noise on our driveway. One of the neighbours, a farmer, had just bought a Model-T Ford. We had never seen an

Above: Julius Shulman's senior year photograph

Left: Yetta Shulman

Facing Page: A young Julius Shulman (far right)

automobile before! That was about 1916 or '17, about the time of World War I. I remember one time an airplane flew over the farm, and the phone began to ring. All the farmers around were asking, 'Did you see the airplane?' What an event for a farm boy in 1917!" [xvi]

Life was basic for the Shulmans. Julius' mother and father worked the farm with one helper. They would occasionally take a three-mile buggy trip to Moosup for fresh meat and fish. His mother would be up at dawn to feed and water their chickens – Rhode Island Reds – collect eggs, milk the cows, bake bread on their six-burner wood and coal stove, and then prepare breakfast for the family of seven. His father would be out with the horse ploughing their land and planting corn and potatoes. There was no electricity, of course, just kerosene lamps. They took baths in a tub in the middle of the kitchen, the water heated on the stove. *"The water supply came from a pump on the sink, a hand pump. The toilets were outside. Sears Roebuck catalogs for paper."* [xvii]

This period was to have a powerful impact on the young Julius. He idolised his mother and attributed many of his interests to her, saying that, *"She was a very understanding, wonderful woman"* and, *"We learned a great deal about life from [her]"*. [xviii] The years on the farm also gave him a lifelong passion for the outdoors, for nature, hiking and swimming, which were to influence him and his art for the rest of his life.

It was somewhat inevitable that Max's pioneering spirit would take him to California, initially leaving Yetta and the children on the farm in Connecticut. By 1920, Max had established a dry goods store, called New York Dry Goods, on Temple Street in Los Angeles, and sent for the rest of the family. In September 1920, Yetta and her children crossed the continent by train, a trip that took the family five days. It created an indelible awareness of the expanse and diversity of the American landscape on ten-year-old Julius. Later, he was to credit his rural small farm upbringing with awakening him to the subtle

changes of light and shadow that would influence the course of his life. His eye developed further in California, where gradations from light to dark were more dramatic, and lush desert foliage contrasted sharply with cerulean sky.

The young Julius and his brothers and sisters went to Alpine Street School, near Sunset Boulevard and Figueroa Street. Their father's store was just a few blocks away. In 1922, Shulman's father decided to move New York Dry Goods to a new building on the aptly named Brooklyn Avenue (now Cesar E. Chavez Avenue), in the Jewish neighbourhood of Boyle Heights, at that time the 'Brooklyn of East Los Angeles.' Mexican and gypsy families bought pickles from barrels along Brooklyn Avenue; Hollenbeck Park was nearby, with its lake and beautiful bridge, as was the imposing redbrick façade of the Breed Street Shul synagogue, where Julius had his bar mitzvah.

When he was 12 years old, Julius joined the Boy Scouts and

rediscovered his love of the outdoors. The troop met at a Methodist church in Boyle Heights, on St Louis Street, and camped out on a large plot of land in the Hollywood Hills that had been donated by Arthur Letts, the founder of the Broadway Department Store.[xix] In conversation in 2000 with travel and documentary photographer Mark Edward Harris, Julius, who was already 90, said, *"I still ski; I still go backpacking. My entire life has been associated with the outdoors... I have really learnt from the balanced rhythm of nature."*[xx] Interviewed for *Los Angeles Magazine* shortly before his death in 2009, Julius revealed that:

"Urban life held little interest for him... A Boy Scout, he would pack his rucksack with canned beans and catch the Red Car north. Passing the bungalow courts and Craftsman houses of El Sereno and Pasadena, he would head for the foothills of the San Gabriel Mountains and hike up Mount Wilson. In the evening he'd unroll his blanket and study the shadows and the light."[xxi]

This was to provide the foundation for his life in photography.

In 1923, just three years after his family arrived in Los Angeles, tragedy struck the Shulman household. Max died of tuberculosis aged just 45, leaving Yetta and Julius' siblings to keep the family business going. Shirley was 17; Lee was a couple years younger. Ben was nearly 14. So Julius' three older siblings were considered old enough

to work in the store with their mother. But Yetta saw something special in 13-year-old Julius, and he was made an exception. As a consequence, for the rest of his life he would see entitlement, admiration and independent thought as his birthright.

Shulman become a keen photographer at Roosevelt High School in Boyle Heights, where he took an elective in photography in 11th grade and experimented with his technique, taking photographs of the lake and wooden bridge in Hollenbeck Park. He used the family Eastman Box Brownie, a simple and inexpensive camera introduced by Eastman Kodak in 1900, which originally cost just $1. He developed the roll film in the school darkroom and made his own prints. Along with some rudimentary guidance on dynamic symmetry from a cousin who taught art in Detroit, this was his only 'formal' training in photography.

One of his school assignments was to photograph events at the southern California high schools final track meeting at the Coliseum in May 1927. His teacher warned the young photography students that:

"You can't photograph action with your Brownie box cameras. If any of you have a chance to get or borrow a news type of camera, which has higher speeds to stop the action of sports, try to get that, because you can't do much with a Brownie."[xxii]

Characteristically, Shulman was not easily discouraged, and used his Box Brownie in defiance of his teacher to take a picture as the hurdlers came over the first hurdle towards him. He made an 8x10-inch glossy print in the school lab, astounding his teacher, who gave him an A. The budding photographer had learnt a valuable lesson, which he would recount to his own students for the rest of his life: if you take a picture in action with the action going away from you or coming towards you, it will not be as blurred as it would be going across your field.

Psychology Building University of California, Berkeley, California. 1934

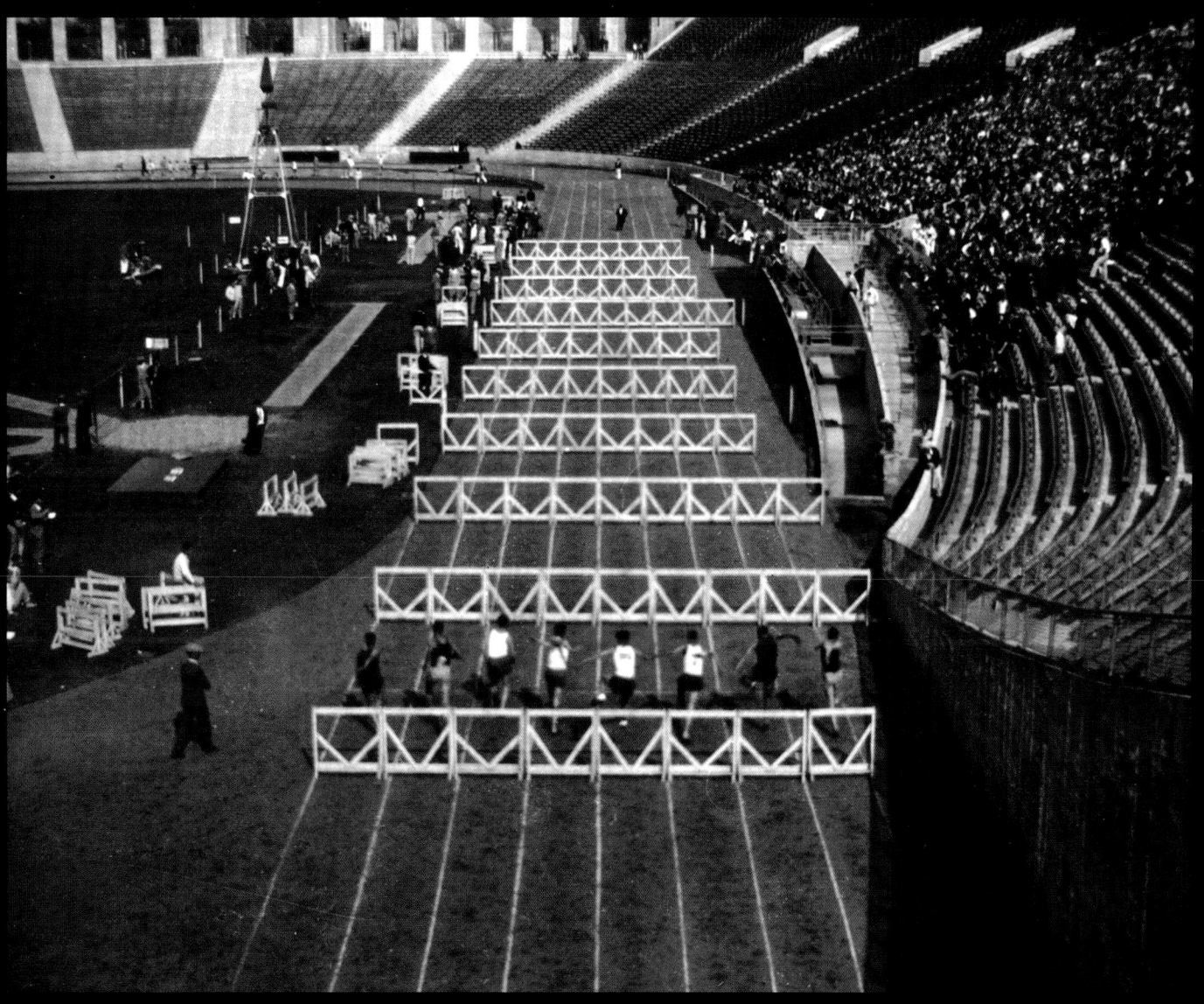

Track Meet Los Angeles, California. 1927

Campanile University of California, Berkeley, California. 1934

In June 1928 Julius graduated from high school and bought his first car, a 1923 Model T Ford, which cost $38. He took a year out of education and in September 1929 enrolled in the Engineering School at the University of California in Los Angeles (UCLA). Although as a hobby he became a ham radio operator and developed an interest in all things electrical, he dropped out of his electrical engineering course after two weeks. Julius drifted between departments, trying out many courses, searching in vain for a subject to capture his interest.

Five years later, Milton Goldberg, a friend from UCLA, enrolled in a Master's degree at the University of California at Berkeley. He encouraged Julius to follow him and two more years of unfocused study ensued. Even though in 1931 he had acquired his own 2Ð×3Ð-inch camera, Shulman had temporarily lost interest in photography. But the year that he enrolled at Berkeley, he was given a Kodak Vest Pocket camera as a 23rd birthday gift. In between classes at Berkeley, Shulman started to take photographs again and set up a darkroom in his shared apartment.

He would "develop [his] Kodak negatives and make 8x10-inch prints of the old buildings on the campus and sell them at the bookstore."[xxiii] The proceeds – at $2.50 per print – supplemented his rent, which was only $25 per month, split with his room-mate. It allowed him to spend much of his day in the gym, swimming and playing basketball or wandering around the campus.

Shulman photographed the Campanile at Berkeley from the arched windows of the Hearst Mining Building and it was printed full page in the *Daily Bruin* (UCLA's university newspaper), his first published architectural photograph. Other early recognition of his talents came in 1933 when he was awarded first place in a photography contest judged by celebrated photographer Margaret Bourke-White (1904–1971). His love of the outdoors, hiking and the landscapes of the California coast inspired his photography. He took his camera on camping trips to Yosemite National Park and the Mojave Desert. He also began to photograph roadways, bridges, and dams, documenting the state of California as it evolved around him.

In 1936, however, Julius asked himself *"What am I doing here? I've been going to college for seven years, I have no major and no idea*

Mount Hollywood Los Angeles, California. 1933

Kun House Los Angeles, California. 1936
Architect: Richard Neutra

what I want to do with my life." [xxiv] He returned to Los Angeles and met a young draftsman, newly arrived from Washington, DC, who was working in Neutra's architectural office and renting a room from Shulman's sister, Shirley Baer. He took Shulman to see Neutra's nearly-completed Kun House on Fairfax near Hollywood Boulevard. The six photographs of the house that Shulman made with his Kodak Vest Pocket camera impressed Neutra to such an extent that he enquired if he could meet the photographer and order some prints.

So Shulman drove to Silver Lake and met Neutra. On examining the 8x10-inch glossy prints that Shulman had made from the Kun House negatives, Neutra asked if he was a professional photographer or studying to become an architect. Shulman replied that he was neither; at the time he had no ambitions to be a photographer or an architect. At any rate, Neutra was suitably impressed and invited Shulman to photograph other projects that he was designing. Suddenly, Shulman was a professional commercial photographer.

"March 5, 1936 — I remember the day — we shook hands for the first time," Shulman said in an interview with the Los Angeles Times. *"I met Richard Neutra, and that was the day I became a photographer."* [xxv]

Shulman had never met an architect before; neither had he ever seen modern architecture like this. Neutra was already established as a successful and enlightened architect, adapting the International Style for West Coast living. The November 1934 issue of *Progressive Contractor* magazine described him as "America's best known architect." [xxvi] So he was well placed to give Shulman a start in life and to mentor him through the early years of his photographic career. Shulman would always recognise what a lucky break his meeting with Neutra had been and how it had directed the course of his life.

Soon after meeting in 1936, Neutra identified something new in Shulman's photographs. He was drawn by Shulman's ability to depict his houses as 'machines for living' in the unique context of the Californian landscape. He realised that Shulman could help him to bring his work to the general public by relating architecture to lifestyle. Neutra saw an ability to capture the aesthetic and emotional intention of his designs. Shulman was brilliant at conveying what it was like to occupy a modern house. He did not just communicate the functional and structural details, scale and beauty of the buildings he photographed; he created seductive, compelling images that allowed viewers to imagine themselves in the scene.

Julius Shulman shattered the common misconception that Modernism was cold and calculated. Instead, he personalised the buildings in an attempt to sell the architecture and Californian lifestyle to the viewers. In Shulman, Neutra identified a fresh eye with a clear and authentic grasp of what his mentor required. Julius showed a thorough understanding of the architect's objectives, and his photographs presented his subjects in a narrative style, which made it easy for East Coast and European publishers to use them in their features.

The irascible Neutra also, perhaps, saw a young man whom he could influence and mould to his needs at a lower cost than the established studios. Whatever the rationale, the young photographer and the established architect formed an enduring working relationship that was to last until shortly before the architect's death in 1970. And so the career of one of the twentieth century's great documentary artists was born.

THE ORIGINS OF ARCHITECTURAL PHOTOGRAPHY

Since the birth of photography over 170 years ago, photographers have focused their cameras on architecture. Architecture was the ideal subject matter for early photographers, including Louis Daguerre (1787–1851) and William Henry Fox Talbot (1800–1877). Slow emulsion speeds required long exposure times, and buildings provided static subjects that would not blur the image as human models might.

Many early architectural photographers adopted the 'elevation approach', addressing their subject head on to create a two-dimensional depiction of a three-dimensional structure. They would work from an elevated position from which the camera lens was level with the mid-height of the building, thereby avoiding converging verticals and other distortions. Others used the 'perspective approach', emphasising the three-dimensional qualities of buildings, often photographed from the corner of a building.

For much of the nineteenth century, "architecture looked very much as stand-alone portraiture, characterised by formal composition, rigorously straight verticals, and an elevated perspective – in both the elevation and perspective styles."[xxvii] By the early twentieth century, however, British photographer Frederick H. Evans (1853–1943) was using the perspective style to transcend mere factual representation. Focusing his lens mainly on French and English cathedrals, Evans developed a straightforward, 'perfect' photographic rendering of architecture, his images not retouched or modified in any way. The resulting elegant platinotype photographs addressed space, light and shade, mass and balance.

PHOTOGRAPHY IN THE MACHINE AGE

"**A**rchitecture is the masterly, correct and magnificent play of masses brought together in light. Our eyes are made to see forms in light; light and shade reveal these forms; cubes, cones, spheres, cylinders or pyramids are the great primary forms which light reveals to advantage; the image of these is distinct and tangible within us without ambiguity. It is for this reason that these are beautiful forms, the most beautiful forms. Everybody is agreed to that, the child, the savage and the metaphysician."[xxviii]

Echoing this dictum by Le Corbusier, British architectural photographer and author Eric de Maré (1910–2002) described photography as "building with light", underscoring the symbiotic relationship between architecture and photography. *"The two fields in which the spirit of our age has achieved its most definite manifestations are photography and architecture. Did modern photography beget modern architecture, or the converse?"*[xxix]

The Machine Age demanded not only a new architectural aesthetic, but a new means of recording it and disseminating its conceptual values: photography was the ideal medium. The limited palette of monochrome photography lent itself to the expression of form, structure, texture, light and shade.

San Bernadino Freeway Los Angeles, California. 1933

City Hall and Construction of Union Terminal Los Angeles, California, 1933

In a 1946 article artist Michael Rothstein wrote, "The modern architect imitates the photographer; he builds with lights and shadows, with black and white."[xxx]

Writing in *The Spectator*, Stephen Bayley explained that:

"Architecture is… fundamentally about the management of light and space. Or, at least, that's how architects see it. So photography makes better sense of architecture than any other medium does: there is something congruent between the fixed optical geometry of a camera and the way we perceive buildings." [xxxi]

Indeed, it could be argued that the International Style could not have become established without the photographs that propagated it. From that time on, many architects began to design with photography in mind. As early as 1931, with modern mass media already well established, cultural critic Walter Benjamin pointed out that *"a photograph is able to isolate, define, interpret, exaggerate or even invent a cultural value for a building."* [xxxii]

At the Bauhaus school, Gropius had started to address the problems of how to unite industry and the arts to create an aesthetic that reflected the spirit of the age. Hungarian painter and photographer László Moholy-Nagy (1895-1946) was appointed instructor of the foundation course. The 1923 curriculum covered form, materials and construction – the basis of the Bauhaus educational programme – and marked the school's transformation from more expressionistic leanings to a school of design and industrial integration.

Moholy-Nagy coined the term 'New Vision' for his belief that photography could create a whole new way of seeing the outside world that the human eye could not.[xxxiii]

As ornamentation was reduced in architecture, so materials and texture became the focus for the photographer's lens. Moholy-Nagy saw this in "the precise magic of the

Oakland Bay Bridge under construction San Francisco Bay, California. 1930

Downtown Los Angeles from the Pasadena Freeway Los Angeles, California. 1950

finest texture: in the framework of steel buildings just as much as the foam of the sea."[xxxiv]

In the same year, American Modernist photographer Edward Weston (1886–1958) noted that, *"The camera should be used for a recording of life, for rendering the very substance and quintessence of the thing itself, whether it be polished steel or palpitating flesh."*[xxxv]

Moholy-Nagy thrived on ideas of dynamic progress, of mechanisation, the inherent possibilities of new materials. As he wrote in *Ma* [Today], the avant-garde magazine then being published in Vienna, *"Everyone is equal before the machine. I can use it; so can you. It can crush me; the same can happen to you."* [xxxvi]

His grasp of new technologies was prophetic. He foresaw photography as the art form of the future.

As the discovery of one-point perspective gave creative impetus to the Renaissance, so Moholy-Nagy realised that technical advances in photography and film would transform social and cultural values as the twentieth century progressed. He predicted: "It is not the person ignorant of writing but the one ignorant of photography who will be the illiterate of the future." [xxxvii] Moholy-Nagy went on to be one of the first designers to realise the potential of photography in advertising and commercial art.

After the Nazis came to power in Germany in 1933, Moholy-Nagy moved to England, becoming part

Smoke and Steam 1934

of the circle of émigré artists and intellectuals who based themselves in the London suburb of Hampstead. He lived for eight months in the Isokon building with Gropius and photographed contemporary architecture for the *Architectural Review*. While in England, Moholy-Nagy photographed the recently completed De La Warr Pavilion, whose architect Erich Mendelsohn (1887–1953) was another recent exile from Berlin. He also took photographs for historian Bernard Fergusson's book *Eton Portrait* and poet John Betjeman's *Oxford University Chest*.[xxxviii]

In 1937, Moholy-Nagy moved to Chicago, setting up what would become the Institute of Design, and in 1938 appointed Mies van der Rohe as director of architecture. In 1949 the school became part of the IIT.

In New York, the current vogue in photography was for soft focus, special filters and exotic printing

Boulder Dam Nevada/Arizona. 1936

Eisenstadt House Los Angeles, California. 1939

Shangri-La Apartments Santa Monica, California. 1941
Architect: William E. Foster

processes to imitate the style of paintings and etchings of that time. It was embodied in the work of Alfred Stieglitz (1864–1946) and practitioners of pictorialist photography.

On the other side of the US, however, a group of photographers that included Ansel Adams (1902–1984), Edward Weston (1886-1958), his son Brett Weston (1911–1993), Imogen Cunningham (1883–1976) and Berenice Abbott (1898–1991) represented the West Coast Photographic Movement. Their rejection of the manipulated print would dominate Modernist photographic aesthetics for the next 40 years. This new artistic value in photography was formalised in 1932 by the formation in San Francisco of the f/64 photographic group, which championed purist – or 'straight' – photography in response to pictorialism. The group included Adams, Cunningham, John Paul Edwards (1884–1968), Sonya Noskowiak (1900–1975), Henry Swift (1891–1962), Willard Van Dyke (1906–1986), and Edward Weston.

The term f/64 refers to a small aperture setting on a large-format camera. The smaller the aperture, the greater the depth of field (the amount of distance between the nearest and farthest objects that appear in focus in a photograph). So at f/64, a photograph will be sharp from foreground to background, a characteristic of the group's photography. In addition to sharp focus, straight photography was associated with higher contrast and an aversion to cropping, emphasising the abstract geometric form of its subjects. Its proponents believed that they were creating a language for translating the metaphysical into visual terms, viewed through a particularly Western lens. Moving on from the traditional

subject matter of portraiture, these photographers focused their lenses on machines, factory work, skyscrapers and technical innovations of all kinds.

Although f/64 was dissolved in 1935, both a product and a victim of the financial pressures resulting from the Great Depression, the group's manifesto had a profound influence on West Coast photography. This created the context in which Julius Shulman emerged as a photographer. His photographs showed a thoroughly Modernist eye, which sometimes manifested itself as direct visual references to his great photographic antecedents; examples include his photograph of a nude woman, *Triangulation* (1951), which closely echoes Cunningham's *Triangles* series from 1928 and Edward Weston's nudes of the late 1930s.

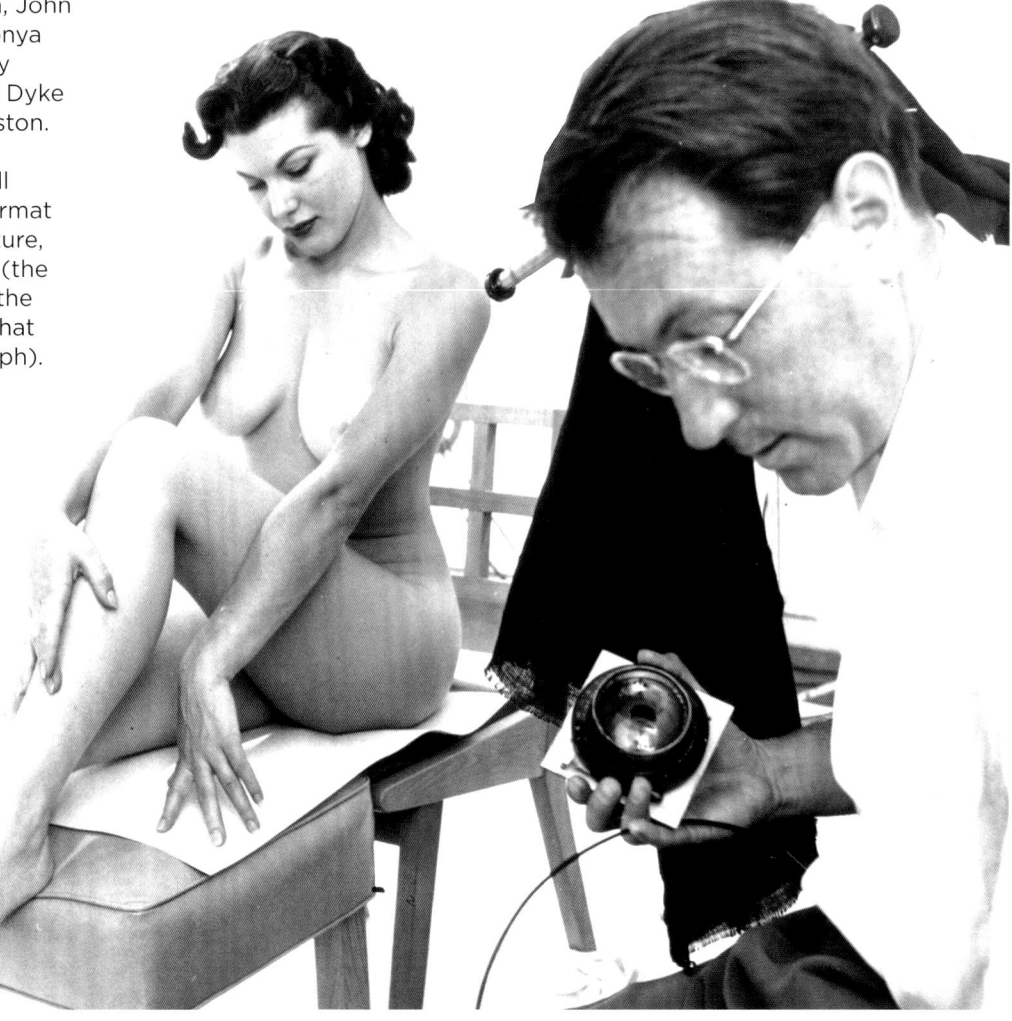

Triangulation, Architectural Nude. 1952

Al's Market Los Angeles, California. 1933

Sixth Street Bridge Los Angeles, California. 1933

Ford Building, Machine Age Exhibition, San Diego, California. 1934

Julius Shulman was not the first architectural photographer. In addition to Moholy-Nagy, Berenice Abbott had focused her lens on the built environment. In 1923, Man Ray (1890–1976) hired Abbott as a darkroom assistant in his portrait studio in Montparnasse, Paris. Abbott returned to her native New York in 1929 with the photographic archive of Eugène Atget (1857–1927). Atget, sometimes described as the grandfather of Modernist photography, had humanised architectural photography and provided a new language that Abbott brilliantly exploited in her own photographs of New York's skyscrapers. She took many of the photographs in Henry-Russell Hitchcock's definitive 1936 book *The Architecture of H.H. Richardson and His Times*,[xxxix] although she is not credited in the book.

Meanwhile, the photographs of Abbott's friend Walker Evans (1903–1975) for the Farm Security Administration depicted the hardship of Depression-era rural communities through his images of modest vernacular architecture. In 1938, Evans was the first photographer to be given a solo exhibition at MoMA. More than half of the images were of architecture.

Hungarian-born photographer André Kertész (1894–1985) and Margaret Bourke-White had also developed a language for photographing architecture before Shulman. Bourke-White's architectural photos were published in several issues of *House & Garden* in 1928 and *Architectural Forum* in 1931.

New York-based F.S. Lincoln (1894–1976), one of America's foremost architectural photographers, produced a body of work during the 1930s and 1940s that documented the influence of the International Style and Art Deco on New York City architecture. Also working in New York, Ezra Stoller's (1915–2004) work featured landmarks of modern architecture, including Mies van der Rohe's Seagram Building, Frank Lloyd Wright's Fallingwater, Alvar Aalto's

(1898–1976) Finnish Pavilion at the 1939 New York World's Fair, and Eero Saarinen's (1910–1961) final project, Bell Labs Holmdel Complex. Stoller is often cited as aiding the spread of the Modernist movement and in 1961 the AIA awarded him its first Gold Medal for Photography.

Ken Hedrich (1929–1971), of Chicago photographic firm Hedrich-Blessing, further advanced the photography of modern architecture. And in California, Neutra worked with Luckhaus Studios and Willard D. Morgan (1900–1967) before meeting Shulman in 1936.

Jewish Community Center
Los Angeles, California. 1938

Fred R. Dapprich (1880–1965) was active in southern California between 1900 and the 1930s, working with Schindler and some of the other early Modernist architects, including Harris. However, his soft, painterly photography, often printed in sepia tones, owed more to the romanticism of the pictorialists than the linear qualities of the Modernists.

Maynard Parker (1900–1976) was a Los Angeles-based architectural and garden photographer who contributed images to many of the nation's premiere home design publications. By 1940 Parker had come to the attention of Elizabeth Gordon, the editor of *House Beautiful*, and thus began an important affiliation that lasted well into the 1960s. Parker came to know a number of leading architects, designers, and builders both through his relationship with *House Beautiful* and through his architect neighbour Harwell Harris. Parker's archive of approximately 58,000 negatives, transparencies, and photographic prints as well as office records and business correspondence is housed at the Huntington Library in San Marino, California.

Other notable contemporary architectural photographers working in the US at the time included:

W.P. Woodcock, who photographed for Schindler, Joseph Eichler (1900–1974), Cliff May (1909–1989) and Harris;

Roger Sturtevant (1903–1982), who received the AIA's architectural photography medal in 1960. He photographed new works in the San Francisco Bay Area from the 1930s through to the 1950s, including those by Modernist landscape architect Thomas Church, and Second Bay Tradition-style architect William Wurster (1895–1973);

Ulrich Meisel, who worked as an architectural photographer in Dallas;

Pedro E. Guerrero (1917–2012), a Mexican-American photographer who worked for Wright and later photographed midcentury modern interiors and the work of artists Alexander Calder (1898–1976)

and Louise Nevelson (1899–1988). He also photographed homes and interiors for *Home & Garden* magazine for 20 years.

In Europe, Le Corbusier had discovered the work of photographer Lucien Hervé (1929–2007). Hervé worked closely with his architect clients to create series of images to portray the spirit of places rather than of actual buildings. He collaborated with Finnish architect, designer, sculptor and painter Aalto, and Brazilian-born architect Oscar Niemeyer (1907–2012), and is known for his beautiful images of Chandigarh, India, Brasilia, Brazil, and Le Thoronet, France. His characteristic style of cropped frames, oblique points of view, and stripped-down, abstracted compositions distinguish his work from that of his contemporaries.

German avant-garde and commercial photographer Ilse Bing (1899–1998) made a series of classic photographs of Dutch Modernist architect Mart Stam's (1899–1986) architecture in Frankfurt, Germany. Moving from

Frankfurt in 1930 to join the burgeoning avant-garde and surrealist scene of Paris in 1930, she subsequently earned the title "Queen of the Leica" from the critic and photographer Emmanuel Sougez (1889–1972) for being the only professional in Paris to use an advanced Leica camera at the time. In 1937 she travelled to New York where her images were included in the landmark exhibition 'Photography 1839–1937' at MoMA. She eventually moved to the US in 1941.

But Shulman's architectural photography stood alone in technique and vision. Painstakingly composed, lit and staged, artfully manipulated in the darkroom, Shulman's images not only fulfilled the architects' requirements for a well-crafted document of a building, but also brilliantly communicated the model for southern California living. His images helped to bring the work of the early West Coast Modernist architects to the general public, relating architecture to lifestyle and simultaneously creating enduring works of art.

SHULMAN'S CAREER DEVELOPS

Having met Shulman in 1936, Neutra promptly introduced the budding architectural photographer to other architects working within the International Style including, among others, his old partner R.M. Schindler, Ain, J.R. Davidson (1889–1977) and Raphael Soriano. Having recently left Neutra's practice, Soriano was just completing his first house, the Lipetz House in Silver Lake, a residential neighbourhood in Los Angeles, California. The introduction from Neutra secured a commission for Shulman, and by the end of 1936 he was an established member of the West Coast architectural photographers' fraternity, managing a constant flow of commissions.

In 1937 Shulman met Schindler at his studio and left with a commission to photograph the recently completed Fitzpatrick House perched at the top of Laurel Canyon in the Hollywood Hills. Schindler continued Shulman's photographic education with a valuable critique of his photographic technique. While reviewing Shulman's prints of his Daugherty House in Santa Monica, he asked why Shulman had illuminated all the interior walls with the same light value. He then showed Shulman the naturally illuminated walls in the studio in the Kings Road House and pointed out how the light fell differently on each one. From then on, Shulman used his electric lights to emulate daylight, giving natural values to interior compositions.

Shulman embarked on his new career at the end of the Depression. Budgets were usually very tight, and designs were simple, even

Below and right: **Lipetz House**
Los Angeles, California. 1939
Architect: Raphael Soriano
(pictured below left)

Fitzpatrick House Los Angeles, California. 1937
Architect: Rudolph Schindler

Fitzpatrick House Los Angeles, California. 1937
Architect: Rudolph Schindler

primitive. There were rarely funds for furniture, draperies or carpeting, and landscaping was often minimal. It required considerable ingenuity to make an engaging photograph in these circumstances, particularly one that would entice publishers to include them in their magazine features. But Shulman excelled at bringing often rather drab subjects to life. He departed from the photography of his predecessors and contemporaries by emphasising light and shade, using dramatic single-point perspective to accentuate volume rather than mass and exploring the texture of building materials.

Shulman provided his architect clients with the visual distinction that they needed to attract attention on the world architectural stage. Neutra was not only a great architect, he was also a consummate self-publicist. Shulman's photographs allowed him to communicate his

architectural ideas in the US and in Europe, extending his reputation on a global stage. In turn, the publication of Shulman's photographs of Neutra designs in a multitude of home and trade magazines promoted the photographer as well.

One of Shulman's earliest publishing successes was with his photographs of the Grace Miller House in Palm Springs. Neutra had designed the house for St. Louis socialite Grace Lewis Miller in 1937. Over three years, from 1936 to 1939, Shulman and Neutra spent many days at the site of the desert residence. Shulman recalled:

"...as the seasons changed and the landscape evolved, we were constantly discovering new moods... Mrs Miller was adept at expressing her observations of my photographs."

Below: Interior of the Fitzpatrick House

Miller House Palm Springs, California. 1937
Architect: Richard Neutra

Miller House Palm Springs, California. 1937
Architect: Richard Neutra

Above: Additional Miller House images with handwritten commentary by Mrs. Miller

"Many of my earliest archival prints have inscribed notes in which she analysed my compositions. How fortunate for a beginner in photography to receive such constructive comments."[xl]

Mrs. Miller's notes inspired a marked improvement in Shulman's compositions and printing techniques and, on publishing an article on the house in 1941, *House Beautiful* magazine declared it 'the best desert house in North America', a reflection, perhaps, as much of Shulman's photographs of the house as of Neutra's design.[xli]

Shulman honed his skills in collaboration with Neutra and his circle. The Depression had left most architects with few commissions, and Neutra could afford to be generous with his time on site, guiding his young protégé through the shoot. No one was hurried, and the resulting images were collaborations between architect and photographer, expressing architectural intention and artistic interpretation.

In 1943, the Second World War interrupted Shulman's career, and he joined the US Army. Shulman spent the final two years of the war as an army hospital photographer at Baxter General Hospital in Spokane, WA, using his 4x5-inch Graphic View camera to photograph surgery. He also continued to pursue his passion for hiking and the outdoors, photographing patients recovering from their war injuries among the beautiful lakes and forests of Washington state.

In 1937, Shulman had married Emma Romm. While Julius was away contributing to the war effort, Emma – who was living with her mother at the time to save costs – put his well-organised archives to work. At the time, MoMA in New York was building up its collections of contemporary architecture. In exchange for glossy prints, printed up by a friend who had a darkroom, MoMA's patronage provided a good second income to supplement the private's pay of $32 a month.

By the time he was discharged from the army as a sergeant in October 1945, Julius was the father of a six-month-old daughter, Judy. He returned to Los Angeles and revived his career as an architectural photographer, reuniting with many of his pre-war clients. The privations of the Depression and the war had meant that funding had been diverted away from house-building and there was now a severe housing shortage. As GIs returned home from the war, construction of low-cost, practical housing was a priority and work was plentiful.

New materials, developed during the war, were used for construction. One of Shulman's first commissions after the war was for architect Edward Larrabee Barnes (1915–2004) who, with industrial designer Henry Dreyfuss (1904–1972), had designed prefabricated homes using aluminium aviation components. In 1947 the Consolidated Vultee company of California, wishing to convert its aircraft plants to produce prefabricated houses, commissioned Dreyfuss and Barnes to work with its aeronautical engineers on the design of a two bedroom unit. The design they came up with was particularly suited to southern California. It was to be manufactured from panels consisting of a kraft paper honeycomb core faced with sheet aluminium, and to be completed on site by conventional tradesmen. Shulman recorded the whole process, from design through manufacture to completion of fully furnished, landscaped houses.

Shulman, who had worked on his own before the war, printing up 10x8-inch glossy prints in his darkroom between commissions, now hired two assistants to help him manage the volume of work that was coming to his studio. In 1949, he was joined by Julius Frank, who did all of his black and white printing until his death of a heart attack in 1959, when Frank's wife, Hildegard, took over, continuing to print for Shulman until 1986.

Vintage Coalyard Spokane, Washington. Photo taken in 1944, during Julius Shulman's time working as an army photographer.

Academy Theater Inglewood, California. 1940
Architect: S. Charles Lee

Mayfair Theater Ventura, California. 1940
Architect: S. Charles Lee

THE SHULMAN HOUSE

Shulman House Los Angeles, California. 1951
Architect: Raphael Soriano

In 1948, Shulman commissioned his friend and client Raphael Soriano to build a house and studio in the Hollywood Hills off Mulholland Drive, into which he, Emma and Judy eventually moved on 5 March 1950. It was 14 years to the day after he first met Neutra and his career began as a photographer.

The framework for the house was fabricated out of steel I-beams. Soriano was an early advocate of building steel-framed homes, allowing the Shulman House to remain largely unaffected by southern California's frequent earthquakes. Massive sliding glass doors opened onto the lush California landscape. The walls were formed of stucco and corrugated steel painted the ochre of weathered brick, and the hallway was lined with cork tiles.

Many of Shulman's circle would have wondered why he had hired Soriano rather than his mentor Neutra. Having worked closely with the autocratic Neutra for a decade, though, Shulman knew that it was unlikely that he would get much say in the design of his own house if he gave Neutra his commission. Soriano, on the other hand, was happy for Shulman and Emma to contribute their own ideas to the design of the house.

Shulman also eschewed the typically sombre and austere interiors of Neutra's purist architecture, advocating instead that homes should be homely and comfortable places in which to live.

He was very particular about the requirement for a proper working kitchen for his family. As many of the architects that he might have considered to design his house were young bachelors, they were very often not successful with their kitchen designs, knowing little about the workings of that part of the house. So Shulman closely oversaw and contributed to Soriano's design of the room.

Shulman also had other requirements of his house: it was to have a fully working studio with darkrooms where he and his assistants could work, next to but separate from the main house, and should include screened porches to anchor the house to its site.

In keeping with Shulman's love of the outdoors, with the help of landscape designer Garrett Eckbo (1910–2000), he and his family developed lush, unrestrained landscaping – some would say jungle – in the two-acre

Above and left: Shulman House Los Angeles, California. 1951
Architect: Raphael Soriano

(0.8 hectare) plot. Boulder-edged trails picked their way through dense eucalyptus and a riot of impenetrable, verdant jade and agave plants to koi ponds; and bobcats, birds, squirrels, lizards and other critters would join Shulman, Emma and Judy during al fresco breakfasts in the screened porches. Shulman planted hundreds of trees and shrubs during the 59 years that he lived there, and redwood trees, now 100 feet (30 metres) tall, frame the hillside behind the house.

Shulman exploited his own house as subject matter for photographic assignments. According to architectural historian John Crosse,[xlii] Shulman's log book reveals that his house was photographed at least 13 times for a variety of clients. The first assignment was Job No. 706, 25 July 1950, for Glide Windows. The cover image on Wolfgang Wegener's Raphael Soriano monograph also appears to be from this session.

Above: Shulman House under construction
Below: Gardens of the Shulman House

In August 1987, at the request of architectural historian Esther McCoy (1904–1989), the City of Los Angeles Cultural Heritage Commission made the house Historic-Cultural Monument #325, the only unaltered steel-frame house by Soriano.

Shulman was to live and work there for the remainder of his life. He would receive visitors and hold meetings in the studio, parked behind his desk where a red telephone rang frequently with new assignments and requests for speaking engagements or interviews.

"A wonderful mess" was how Shulman described his desk. Interspersed among the family snapshots, mementos, and tchotchkes were several enlarged quotations, including one from *Art News*: "*If buildings were people, those in Julius Shulman's photographs would be Grace Kelly: classically elegant, intriguingly remote.*"[xliii]

FROZEN MUSIC?
UNDERSTANDING THE ROLE OF ARCHITECTURAL PHOTOGRAPHY

Since the sixth century BC, the connection between music and architecture has been thought to be united by a common code. Mathematicians and geometrists revealed the underlying order of this connection. Greek philosopher and mathematician Pythagoras (c. 570–495 BC) was credited with deciphering the code, leading to many Greek temples being designed along proportional principles that revealed not only supreme beauty but "the music of the heavenly spheres".[xliv]

Bayley wrote, "*Everyone knows about architecture being frozen music. The source of that conceit may be debated, but its validity is timeless and certain. For all its weightiness, architecture plays with ethereal proportion, harmony, resonance and delight: the stuff of music.*"[xlv]

As a review in *Architectural Record* put it, "*The best architecture photographers use light and perspective to elevate what could be static images into single-frame movies, documenting places as organisms full of verve, mystery, and life.*"[xlvi]

Whether reflecting frozen music or creating single-frame movies, the photographer must have a deep understanding of and sympathy for designers and engineers. The job of architectural photographers is to reproduce the essential elements of a three-dimensional, functional structure in two dimensions. So, they must transcend the mere physical role of recording. As Shulman put it, "*Photographers bear a responsibility – we recreate a structure's role in the history of architecture.*"[xlvii]

To fulfil this responsibility, architectural photographers

Maslon House Rancho Mirage, California. 1963
Architect: Richard Neutra

Firestone Tire and Rubber Company Headquarters Los Angeles, California. 1958
Architect: William L. Pereira and Associates

require some rare qualities: they must combine an instinct for the architect's intentions with a sense of drama and the ability to communicate the purpose and mood of a building.

It is not always a literal translation. In his introduction to Shulman's book *Photographing Architecture and Interiors*, Neutra wrote:

"Architecture is NOT frozen music...! It plays on us in time, the vivid time of our living responses which melt one moment into the next, and one impression into what follows, while we minutely move the eye, turn and tilt the head, or step through spaces and past form." [xlviii]

The photographer must catch this fleeting spirit: Shulman would plan his shoots impeccably, watching the way that the sun created shadows and revealed texture. Carefully, though sometimes instinctively, Shulman would choose what the French pioneer of street photography Henri Cartier-Bresson (1908–2004) described as "the decisive moment". [xlix] Shulman believed that all photography is timing. Shadows delineate structures and give them dimension. [l]

Describing his technique, Shulman said, "*We relate to the position of the sun every minute of the day.*" Holding a photograph of an Oakland 1910 Craftsman-style house by Bernard Maybeck (1862–1957) to the lamp on his desk, he continued:

"So when the sun moves around, we're ready for our picture. I have to be as specific as a sports photographer – even a little faster. This is early afternoon, when the sun is just hitting the west side of the building. If I'm not ready for that moment, I lose the day."

He did not, however, need to observe the light before photographing: "*I was a Boy Scout – I know where the sun is every month of the year. And I never use a meter.*" [li]

He applied what he called the 'four Ts':

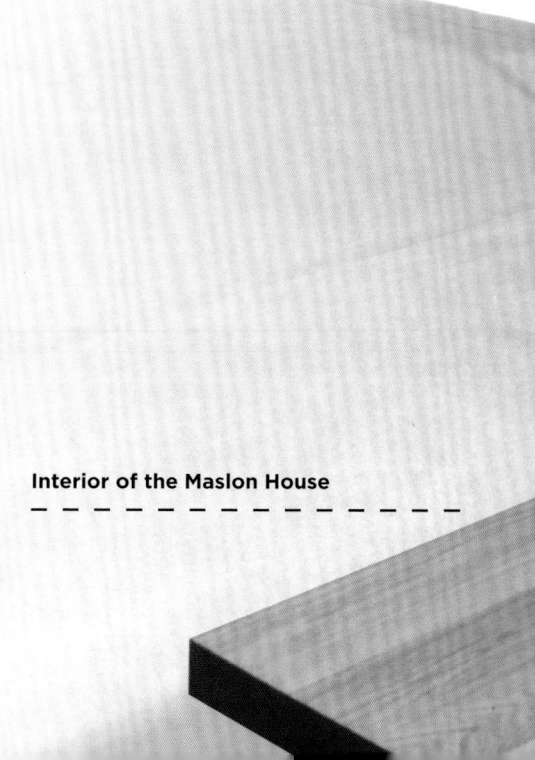

"Transcend is, I go beyond what the architect himself has seen. Transfigure – glamorise, dramatise with lighting, time of day. Translate – there are times, when you're working with a man like Neutra, who wanted everything the way he wanted it – 'Put the camera here.' And after he left, I'd put it back where I wanted it, and he wouldn't know the difference – I translated. And fourth, I Transform the composition with furniture movement." [lii]

To illustrate the latter, Shulman often demonstrated with an interior of the Abidi House (2004), designed by James Tyler, former principal architect for Craig Ellwood and now Adjunct Professor at USC School of Architecture. The photograph looks out from the living room, through a long glass wall, to the grounds. Shulman explained in an interview for *Dwell* magazine in 2009:

"Almost every one of my photographs has a diagonal leading you into the picture," he says. Taking a notecard and pen, he draws a

Interior of the Maslon House

line from the lower left corner to the upper right, then a second perpendicular line from the lower right corner to the first line. Circling the intersection, he explains, *"That's the point of what we call 'dynamic symmetry'."* When he holds up the photo again, I see that the line formed by the bottom of the glass wall – dividing inside from outside – roughly mirrors the diagonal he's drawn. Shulman then indicates the second, perpendicular line created by the furniture arrangement. *"My assistants moved [the coffee table] there, to complete the line. When the owner saw the Polaroid, she said to her husband, "Why don't we do that all the time?"'* [liii]

Shulman considered the camera to be the least important element in photography. *"Don't act like a photographer, act like a human being reviewing a piece of sculpture"* [liv], he would expound. But Shulman never ignored the technology behind his images. In fact, he was a master in the use of camera, lenses and creative lighting, using technique to emphasise form and texture. He also understood the contribution that darkroom manipulation could make to the final image, producing impeccable prints whose subtle tonal range communicated the nuanced gradation of materials and light as it might be experienced by the person occupying the architectural space.

Shulman possessed abundant energy and enthusiasm for his work, and developed a unique style of carefully composed and artfully lit house portraits, which quickly established him as the pre-eminent architectural photographer on the West Coast. His photographs reflected his own optimism and love of nature, epitomising the idyllic sunny, suburban California lifestyle.

Neutra, always in a hurry, would want his houses photographed before they were finished, certainly before they were landscaped. Shulman saw the significance of context, frequently arranging branches cut from nearby trees to give the impression that the yard had been landscaped, even if it was still a building site. On one assignment, Shulman photographed one of Cliff May's low-cost $12,000 tract houses for *Good Housekeeping* magazine. When Shulman arrived at the house, there was no landscaping:

"[I] went to the nursery and rented some canned plants – five gallon cans of roses and geraniums, whatever they had in bloom – and set them up in front of the house and framed the picture with these plants, and we broke off a branch from a walnut tree that was growing nearby and fastened the branches to a lightstand so we could frame the

Julius Shulman photographing the Cliff May House. Note the carefully arranged foliage.

Cliff May House West Covina, California. 1954
Architect: Cliff May

picture with an arching branch to look like there was a tree there. And in the finished pictures, the house is perfectly landscaped."[lv]

The magazine's architectural interior editor, Mary Kraft, was delighted with the results.

Julius also liked to tell the story of another assignment, this time for Ellen Sheridan, one of the editors of *House & Garden* magazine who had commissioned him to photograph an azalea garden in Pasadena. The weather delayed the shoot, and by the time they got there, the azaleas had died. Never being defeated by this sort of a challenge, Julius made replacement azalea blossoms out of Kleenex tissues. When the photograph was published, no one could tell the difference.

Shulman would also turn up to photograph newly constructed houses with his car loaded with props and furniture, often from his own house, which he would arrange to make the residence appear lived-in and homely. This often exasperated architects who wished to present a more contrived, minimal interior, in tune with their Modernist archetype. Neutra, in particular, sought to present a newly constructed home with minimal furniture when it was photographed for a magazine spread. This often caused some tension between the architect and Julius Shulman, who sought to humanise the houses he photographed by including the trappings of real family life to soften Neutra's austere interior architecture.

On one occasion in 1963, Neutra had asked Shulman to photograph the newly completed Maslon House at the Tamarisk Country Club in Cathedral City near Palm Springs.

Shulman was indignant at Neutra's insistence that most of the furniture and all of the fine art collection – which included masterworks by Henri Matisse, Joan Miró and Alberto Giacometti – should be removed from the shot. But in a typical show of assertiveness, behind Neutra's back Shulman sought – and gained – permission from the owners, Samuel and Luella Maslon, to return two weeks later to re-photograph the house the way he wanted it. The resulting images were much more human and alluring and showed the forceful nature of the photographer.

Shulman often urged his students:

"Those of you who hope to be architects, please be human about how people live in your house. Don't wipe it clean and empty the way Neutra used to do it, because he was more interested in the image of a house – pure architecture, without furniture."[lvi]

Maslon House (photographed without Neutra) Rancho Mirage, California. 1963
Architect: Richard Neutra

THE ARCHITECTURAL PHOTOGRAPHER'S TOOLBAG

There is only you and your camera. The limitations in your photography are in yourself, for what we see is what we are.[lvii]
Ernst Haas (1921–1986)

Actually, it was less of a tool bag and more of a truckload! In the pre-digital era, an architectural photographer's equipment was extremely bulky. Small cameras, such as Shulman's beloved Kodak Vest Pocket camera on which he had produced his first architectural photographs for Neutra, used a small negative of just $2^{5/8}$ x $1^{3/4}$ inches. When the photograph was enlarged to the standard 10x8-inch print, it could be a bit grainy, having lost much of its clarity in the process.

The fixed lens of the camera could also be an impediment: it tended to have the disadvantage that the image became distorted if the camera moved away from the horizontal. A typical example of this is the 'converging verticals' experienced when photographing a tall building if the camera is tilted.

Shulman wrote:

"*To allow maximum expression of architectural interpretation the photographer must use the camera which will a) produce a good negative (or transparency) of adequate size for publication... ; b) achieve good depth of focus; and c) cover the largest visual area possible with the minimum amount of distortion either horizontal or vertical.*" [lviii]

The standard size of a print for reproduction was 8x10 inches, so 8x10-inch or 4x5-inch format view cameras were frequently the chosen equipment for serious photographers. Such cameras incorporate a ground glass viewfinder onto which the reversed image is projected from the lens. The photographer uses this for focusing and composition. As the ground glass is the same size as the negative sheet film, the photographer can check all the elements of the image with great attention to detail before exposure.

The large format means that there is little loss of quality (grain) when enlarging to 8x10 inches and their mechanical design gives the photographer the ability to compensate for distortion: with most large-format cameras, the back and front elements can be moved independently of one another. As Shulman himself explained:

"The back can be swung on a horizontal (and vertical) axis to rectify perspective distortion or achieve depth of field. The lens can be tilted on a horizontal (or vertical) axis for sharp focus. The front can be raised or dropped or moved sideways to get the lens and film in the correct relationship when the subject is not on the same plane as the camera." [lix]

However, 8x10-inch cameras have the disadvantage of being heavy and awkward to handle. They will also record less depth of focus (the distance between the nearest and farthest objects in a scene that appear acceptably sharp in an image) than smaller-format cameras and are much more expensive. As a result, a 4x5-inch plate camera provides a good compromise, even though the negative area is a quarter the size of a 10x8-inch camera.

In the late 1930s, Shulman had graduated from using his Kodak

Vest Pocket camera to using a 4x5-inch plate camera, and even occasionally an Eastman Master View 10x8-inch camera, the first monorail view camera. In 1962, Carl Koch (1916–2005), the designer of the Sinar 4x5-inch camera, gave Shulman two of his cameras and lenses, the brilliant new design turning Shulman's photographic life around, giving him much greater control over image capture. Later, Shulman was also to use a Horseman view camera, as well as a Hasselblad 2Ðx2Ð-inch medium-format camera and Nikon 35mm cameras for personal work.

However, Shulman did not just rely on equipment. Having bought a light meter in 1936, he abandoned it within a year, relying on experience to achieve perfect exposure and preferring to read the light himself. When discussing technique he asserted:

"If you can't interpret light and the way in which it plays with and defines its subjects, if you can't understand the subtle and not-so-subtle rhythms of the sun, if you can't recognise an architect's intent the minute you walk into a room, no amount of money you spend on a camera will make you a photographer."[lx]

Supplementing daylight with artificial light was also important. Having learnt his early lesson from Schindler, Shulman was a master at balancing indoor and outdoor exposures, often using flashbulbs. He would always carry a range of varying strengths: 11, 22 and 50 made by Westinghouse, General Electric and Sylvania.

Ultimately, Shulman's mastery of the use of particular film emulsions, lenses and filters, composition and lighting, timing and darkroom manipulation were all essential elements in producing a successful image.

POPULATING THE PHOTOGRAPH

Before the development of high-speed film emulsions, large-format photography required long exposure times. Any movement during the exposure would result in a blurred image. For this reason, architectural photographers tended to avoid including the human form in their photographs. This explains why many of the first photographs were of buildings, not of people: for example, Fox Talbot's photographs of Lacock Abbey or Daguerre's view of Boulevard du Temple in Paris. Eventually this absence of animated objects in architectural photographs was codified into the genre: if one wanted to be taken seriously as an architectural photographer, one needed to keep people out of the frame.

This attitude remained somewhat unchanged until Julius Shulman came to prominence. Photographers had been hired to illustrate the architectural fundamentals of space, mass, texture and (sometimes) colour, not what a building 'felt' like. Shulman wanted to communicate the lifestyle that could be enjoyed in southern California and its architecture; that modern architecture, far from being stark and sterile, could provide a warm, alluring, glamorous space for living. He often included people in his photographs as 'witnesses', to illustrate how spaces could be

Skinner House Beverly Hills, California. 1959
Architect: Robert Skinner

Convair Astronautics San Diego, California. 1958
Architect: Pereira & Luckman

Baldwin Hills Theater Los Angeles, California. 1950
Architect: Lewis Eugene Wilson

used and to make architecture more accessible and comfortable to the 'average' American home buyer.

Shulman's use of exquisitely balanced lighting showed a profound understanding of the built environment and the relationship between structure, light, shade and setting. He recognised that architecture was for people and was credited with being the first architectural photographer to populate his images with the owners, their friends or their children, and sometimes even the architect's assistants, imparting a human element that made it easy for magazine editors to tell a story. He had a unique ability to document what a building felt like, experientially, as well as what it looked like.

The human figure could also be used to enhance the lighting in a photograph. In his 1947 image of

Neutra's Kaufmann House in Palm Springs, for instance, Shulman strategically placed Mrs. (Liliane) Kaufmann in front of the pool light to prevent it from 'blowing out' the scene. This image was flawlessly crafted, with the house, the pool and the surrounding landscape each exposed separately in an exposure that took 45 minutes.

That Shulman's photographs often appear spontaneous is an illusion. While the photographer worked fast, each image was meticulously set up with composition, lighting and darkroom manipulation all carefully planned ahead of time. Any people who may appear in the frame were intended not only to help the viewer to imagine what it felt like to live in the house but also to show scale without obscuring the view.

Shulman's architectural photography remains unusual and groundbreaking even today. In an

Neutra's Kaufmann House Mrs. Kaufmann is carefully positioned so as to hide any excess flare from the pool light.

Above: Alexander House
Palm Springs, California. 1957
Architect: Palmer & Krisel

Right: Robert L Frost Memorial Auditorium
Culver City, California. 1963
Architect: Flewelling & Moody

article for *Architects' Journal* on communicating the value of design Amanda Spence wrote:

"Flick through any architecture magazine, or scroll through the galleries online, and you will most likely be enticed by photography which shows off the beautiful forms of the latest buildings to be completed. But where are all the people? Architects design places for people. People commission architects to design homes, schools, hospitals and offices; and people use the finished buildings. Yet all too often architectural photography leaves out the people and possessions which fill spaces in everyday life. The sculptural forms of empty buildings might excite other architects, but these bare images do little to communicate the benefits of good architecture to the wider public – something designers are notoriously bad at. In fact, much architectural photography and the language used by architects to talk about their work serve to reinforce the stereotype of the aloof egotist." [lxi]

Los Angeles-based architectural photographer Tim Street-Porter sums up how original this technique was: *"Those photographs, with young, attractive people having breakfast in glass rooms beside carports with two-tone cars, were remarkable in the history of architectural photography. [Julius Shulman] took that to a wonderfully high level."* [lxii]

Palm Springs Aerial Tramway Valley Station Palm Springs, California. 1964
Architect: Albert Frey

Mobil Station Anaheim, California. 1956

ARTS AND ARCHITECTURE
THE CASE STUDY PROGRAM

One of the earliest and most prolific relationships that Shulman built with a magazine was that with *Arts and Architecture*, to which Esther McCoy regularly contributed. The magazine had given Shulman his final commission before he joined the army, photographing a massive, newly constructed synthetic rubber plant built for Dow Chemical, Shell Oil and US Rubber Co., under the direction of the War Production Board.

In the January 1945 edition of the magazine, editor John Entenza (1905-1984) announced the Case Study House Program. Entenza's goal was to encourage architects to design and build low-cost modern houses for real clients, using industrial materials donated by manufacturers. A key element of the programme was to publish and publicise their efforts, an objective in which Julius Shulman and his camera would be instrumental. The programme aspired to create experimental prototypes for developers to pick up, in anticipation of a building boom following the Depression and the war.

The houses were characterised by flat roofs, glass walls, modular design and steel frame construction. By today's standards, they were modest in size, and neatly integrated into their sites, with an emphasis on indoor-outdoor living. It was hoped that the designs would help boost living standards for low-income families, but the solutions were often costly and unpopular; the abundant use of glass, for instance, was impractical in suburbs where houses were built close to neighbours and roads. As Shulman recollected, "*I listened to people coming through the houses, saying 'I don't want to live in a goldfish bowl.'*"

During the life of the programme, 36 designs were accepted, 26 of

Case Study House #8 Pacific Palisades, California. 1950
Architect: Charles & Ray Eames

Case Study House #8 Pacific Palisades, California. 1950
Architect: Charles & Ray Eames

Case Study House #8 Pacific Palisades, California. 1958
Architect: Charles & Ray Eames

Case Study House #21 Los Angeles, California. 1958
Architect: Pierre Koenig

Case Study House #21 Los Angeles, California. 1958
Architect: Pierre Koenig

which were built, almost all in Los Angeles. The best-known Case Study houses were designed by Charles and Ray Eames (CSH#8), Pierre Koenig (CSH#21 and 22, the Stahl House), Craig Ellwood (CSH#17B, 18B and 1953), Richard Neutra (CSH#20A), and Raphael Soriano (CSH#1950). They reflected the spirit of International Style Modernism, expressed in response to the unique landscape, climate and culture of California.

Julius Shulman was already an established architectural photographer when he first photographed a Case Study house – CSH#3, designed by William Wurster and Theodore Bernardi (1903–1990) – for the March 1949 edition of *Arts and Architecture*. He went on to photograph 18 of them altogether, making a critical contribution to the enduring reputation of the programme and its architects.

The Case Study Program ended in 1966 when *Arts and Architecture* ceased publication. Yet remarkably, 18 Case Study houses are still standing and recognisable. Much of the credit for ensuring that these houses survived the whims of fashion can be attributed to Shulman's images, which have consistently inspired generations of architects, designers, filmmakers and those who aspire to recreate the golden age of 'California Living'. His photographs are just as fresh today as they were 50 years ago and they retain the power to excite and promote preservation.

Despite Entenza's aspiration for the Case Study Program, only one house design was ever replicated. It is ironic, then, that Shulman's photographs of those houses have become the most reproduced architectural images of the twentieth century, helping to mythologise the programme and giving it influence out of all proportion to its success.

Shortly after his photographs of CSH#22 (Stahl House) were published in June 1960, film producers were lining up to use the house as a location and the resulting fees were reported to have repaid the cost of building the house within four years. This architectural icon has remained almost unchanged over the intervening half century, with just a few exceptions: the windows have been replaced with shatter-proof glass; a walkway was constructed around the cantilevered living room to make it easier for the window cleaners; and the Van Keppel-Green furniture which was brought in for the *Arts and Architecture* shoot in 1960 was too expensive for the Stahls to keep. Today the house appears in countless commercials, music videos and fashion shoots, all of which serve to keep the architecture in the public eye.

Buck and Carlotta Stahl lived in their dream house for the remainder of their lives, with their children Bruce, Sharon and Mark enjoying an unorthodox childhood, diving off the flat roof into the pool for coins thrown there by their grandfather and roller skating along concrete floors that extend seamlessly from inside to out.

Case Study House #22 (Stahl House)
Los Angeles, California. 1960
Architect: Pierre Koenig

Case Study House #22 (Stahl House) Los Angeles, California. 1960
Architect: Pierre Koenig

Greene House Norman, Oklahoma. 1961
Architect: Herb Greene

BEYOND CALIFORNIA

The architectural photographer's role is to communicate the architect's intentions to a wider audience, approximating the emotional response to a building through a two-dimensional image. In Shulman's lifetime, photography became the main link between designer and public, and critical for the publication of architects' work.

Throughout his career, Shulman made frequent trips to New York. In the wake of the war, demand increased among East Coast publishers for fresh material. This created a new source of assignments for architectural photographers and Julius Shulman, ever the self-promoter, took full advantage. On Shulman's first trip to New York in 1947 Katherine Morrow Ford hosted a cocktail party for him. Ford was architectural editor of *House & Garden* from 1945 until 1949 and consulting architectural editor from 1949 until 1951. She had published many of Shulman's photographs in the 1940 book *The Modern Home In America*, which she had co-written with her husband Prof. James Ford.[lxiii] At the party she introduced Shulman to many eminent East Coast architects, some of whom he would go on to work for, among them Gropius.

McCoy, who had written for many East Coast magazines, was instrumental in introducing Shulman to their editors, with many of whom Shulman developed close working relationships. As a result, as well as *House & Garden*, Shulman's images appeared in *Ladies' Home Journal*, *Good Housekeeping*, *House and Home*, *Architectural Forum* and many other lifestyle and architectural trade magazines, which helped to promote the work of his architect clients as well as his own.

Shulman's published work allowed him to become known to architects across the country and around the world. He worked in 44 of the 50 States, Canada, South America, Asia, Europe and Israel. Ramey and Himes in Kansas, Crites and McConnell in Iowa, Blaine Drake (1911–1993) in Arizona and Don Polsky (1928–) in Nebraska were all to call on Shulman's photographic services. He also won commissions to photograph modern buildings in Uruguay and Argentina, the works of Ricardo Legoretta (1931–2011) and Abraham Zabludovsky (1924–2003) in Mexico

United Covenant Presbytarian Church
Danville, Illinois. 1972
Architects: Crites & McConnell

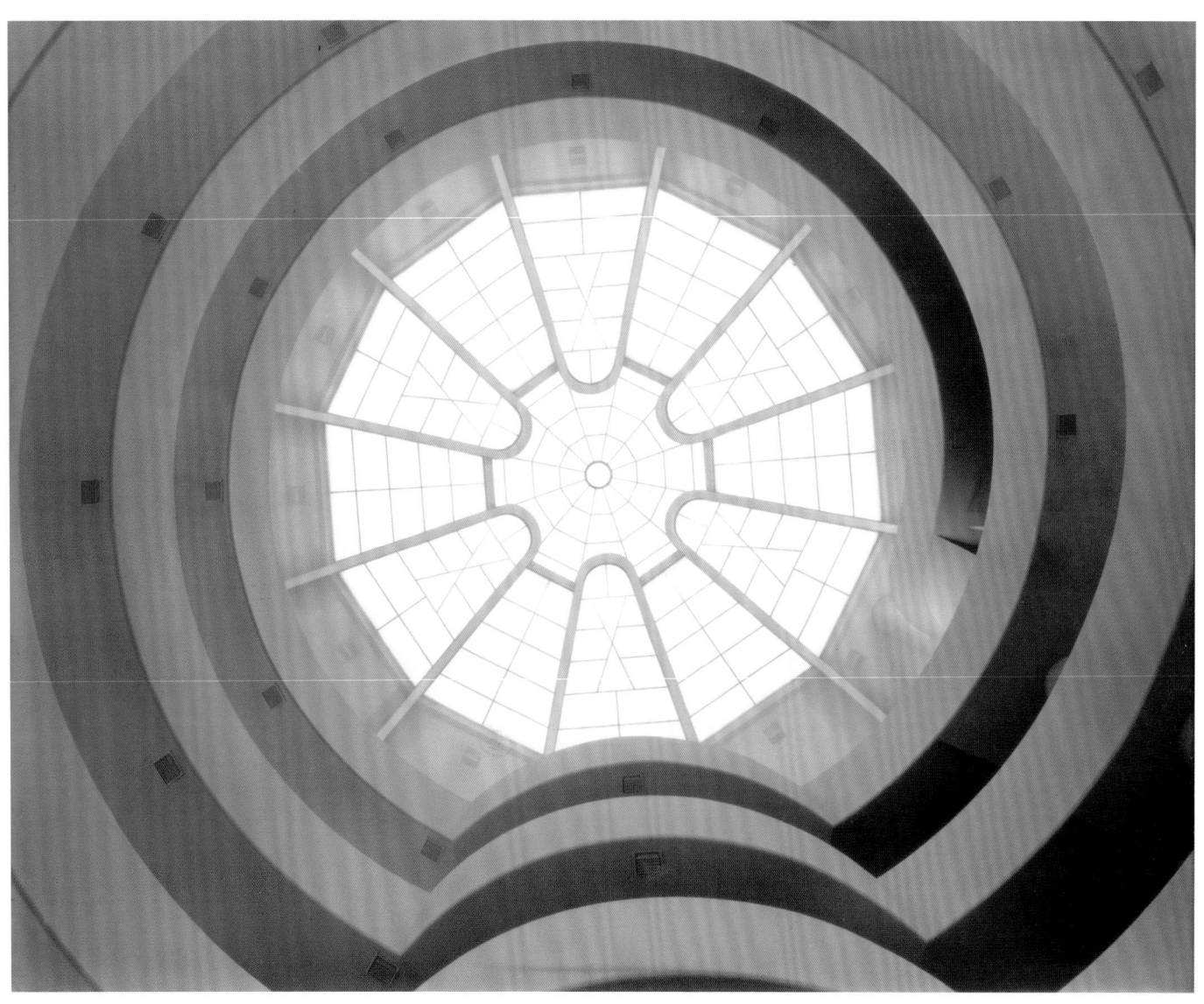

Solomon R. Guggenheim Museum New York, New York. 1959
Architect: Frank Lloyd Wright

Congress Building and Ministries Brasilia, Brazil. 1977
Architect: Oscar Niemeyer

and Brazil, and Henry Moore sculptures in England.

Sometimes Shulman was commissioned by former students. He had met Ray Crites and Dick McConnell as undergraduates at Iowa State University where he was giving a series of lectures, for example. When they graduated and set up their architectural partnership in Cedar Rapids, IA, Shulman began to receive commissions from them.

On one assignment, Shulman photographed seven projects for Crites and McConnell across Iowa. He took the resulting prints to New York, and met over lunch with Doug Haskell, the editor of *Architectural Forum*, executive director Joe Hazen, associate editor Mary Jane Lightbown, and graphic designer and art director Paul Grotz. As a result, all seven houses were published in the magazine, considerably boosting the architects' public profile. Not long after, *Life* magazine chose Crites to represent American architects under the age of 40 in an article they were running.

While photographing for Blaine Drake in Phoenix, AZ, in 1950, Shulman was introduced to Frank Lloyd Wright – by that time 87 years old – and stayed at Taliesin West, the winter home, studio and architectural campus that Wright had begun in 1937 in the beautiful Sonoran Desert in nearby Scottsdale, AZ. Over the course of a week, Shulman discussed architecture with the master architect, gaining insights that would

give Shulman a greater understanding of architectural theory and inform his future work. He also created a portfolio of photographs of Taliesin West, which he later presented to Wright.

Wright went on to commission Shulman to photograph his design for the V.C. Morris shop in San Francisco. The images that Shulman produced prompted Wright to exclaim,

Above: '3 Part Reclining Figure' by Henry Moore

Below: Delegacion Cuauhtémoc
Mexico City, Mexico. 1976
Architect: Abraham Zabludovsky

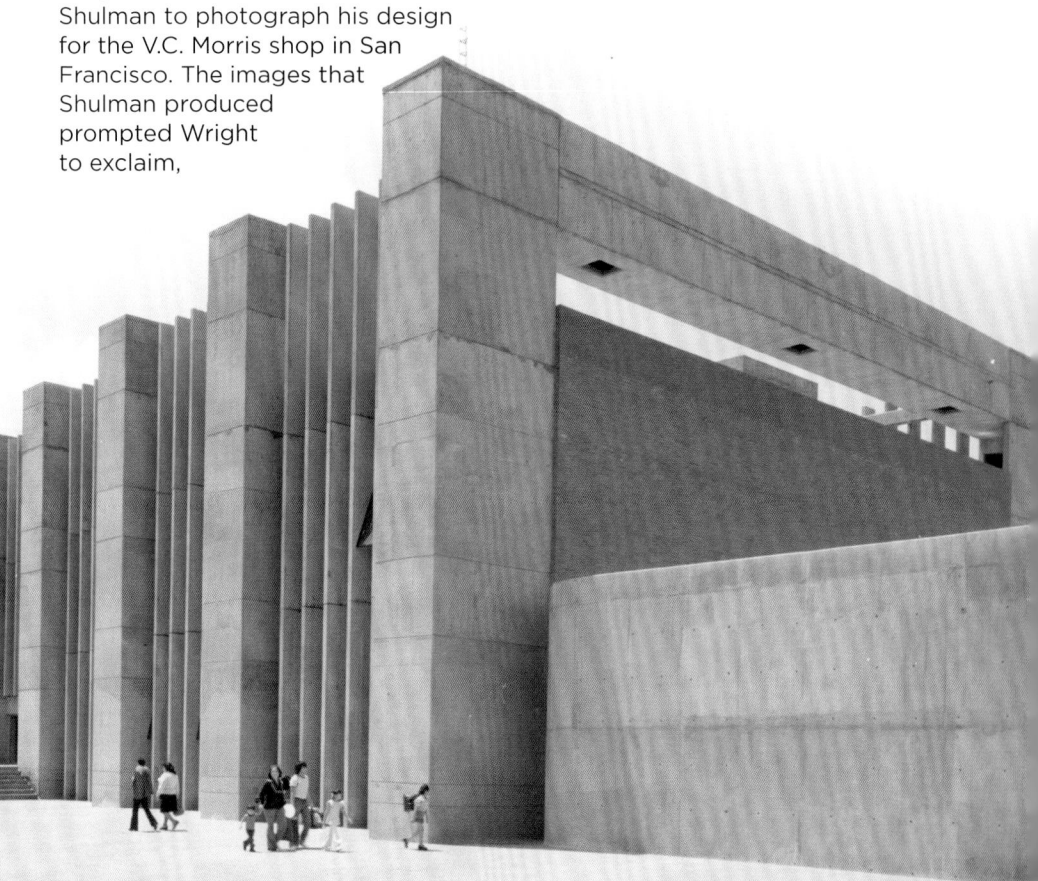

V.C. Morris Shop San Francisco, California. 1951
Architect: Frank Lloyd Wright

"Shulman, at last someone understands, in a photograph, my statement – you have penetrated the spirit of my design!" [lxiv] Shulman continued to work for Wright during the 1950s. He photographed Wright's Freeman, Ennis and Storer textile block houses in southern California – the resulting pictures would appear alongside McCoy's architectural writings – and in 1959 went to New York to photograph the Guggenheim Museum at 1071 Fifth Avenue, which was designed by Wright and completed in the year of his death.

By 1956, Esther McCoy and Shulman had gone further afield, collaborating on a story on Mayan structures for the *Los Angeles Times*. The article included photographs of the Governor's Palace and the Pyramid of the Magician at Uxmal in Yucatán state in Mexico. Shulman and McCoy climbed the temple at Chichén Itzá. Shulman recounted how they:

"...sat there by moonlight. I had set up a camera, and I carried a bag of flashbulbs, and Esther carried an extra bag of bulbs on her back, and I had a flashgun. We walked, and I set the camera on a time exposure in the moonlight, and we walked up to the very top of the temple. But I kept interspersing the walking with firing flash. And the flash shows in the finished photograph. You can see my white shirt, and on one picture, at the very top of the temple, is an image of a person standing near the flashgun, and there's a white, just a blurred white thing, and that's Esther at the very top of the temple. And anyhow, then we sat and talked in the moonlight, just listening to the sounds and quiet of the full moon." [lxv]

Below: Shulman surveying the ruins at Chichén Itzá, Mexico

Ruins and Crafts (Chichén Itzá site) Yucatán state, Mexico. 1956

Ennis House Los Angeles, California. 1952
Architect: Frank Lloyd Wright

Ennis House Los Angeles, California. 1952
Architect: Frank Lloyd Wright

Ennis House Los Angeles, California. 1952
Architect: Frank Lloyd Wright

Ennis House Los Angeles, California. 1952
Architect: Frank Lloyd Wright

Bank of London & South America Buenos Aires, Argentina. 1967
Architect: Testa, Elia & Ramos

Church Atlántida, Uruguay. 1967
Architect: Eladio Dieste

Crites House Cedar Rapids, Iowa. 1964
Architect: Crites & McConnell

PALM SPRINGS AND DESERT MODERNISM

Shulman had been visiting Palm Springs since the 1920s. In 1926, aged 16, he had camped there with teammates from his high school gymnastics team. He would often drive down from Los Angeles in summer, when the desert heat was at its height and Palm Springs was all but abandoned except for small bands of the Agua Caliente tribe, left as caretakers while the rest of their members migrated to cooler climes. Shulman exercised his love of the outdoors, hiking in the majestic canyons around the city, camping near bubbling natural hot springs at the site of what is now the Palm Springs Spa and Hotel.

The steep San Jacinto Mountains to the west of Palm Springs protect the city from coastal fog, rain and smog, creating an other-worldly sanctuary in the middle of the desert. Seemingly unlimited land, a good supply of spring water from an underground aquifer, mineral hot springs and clean dry air attracted settlers in search of a healthy climate from the late nineteenth century.

Desert Hot Springs Motel
Desert Hot Springs, California. 1949
Architect: John Lautner

Oasis Building Palm Springs, California. 1953
Architect: Williams, Williams & Williams

But it was film executives in the 1920s and 1930s, looking for good locations outside Los Angeles, who first brought Palm Springs and the Coachella Valley to the attention of Hollywood's glitterati. The area quickly became a popular escape: accessible from Los Angeles and styled as a Californian Shangri-La, the wealthy and famous transformed it into their own desert playground. Tennis clubs, spas, cocktail lounges and resort hotels were built to accommodate their tastes for luxury and entertainment, and the town flourished during winter months.

Many celebrities stayed and purchased hideaway homes in Palm Springs, including Frank Sinatra, Dean Martin, Sammy Davis, Jr., George Hamilton, Bob Hope, Albert Einstein, Bing Crosby, Kirk Douglas, Cary Grant and Jack Benny. The Hollywood stars were followed by businessmen looking to escape harsh East Coast winters. So it was a rich market for well-travelled architects looking for undeveloped spaces in which to experiment with the International Style aesthetic.

Whereas modern architecture thrived in Los Angeles, partly as a result of the flourishing film industry, very few modern buildings had been built in Palm Springs. Schindler had built the Popenoe Cabin (1922); Frank Lloyd Wright had designed the Oasis Hotel (1923); Prairie School architect William Gray Purcell (1880–1965), a disciple of Louis Sullivan, built his own house there (in 1933); and Neutra had built the Miller House (1937). But essentially, before the Second World War, Palm Springs was virgin territory for modern architects.

Above: Tennis Club Palm Springs, California. 1947
Architect: A. Quincy Jones & Paul R. Williams

Below: Desert Hot Springs Motel Desert Hot Springs, California. 1949
Architect: John Lautner

Palm Springs City Hall Palm Springs, California. 1958
Architect: Clark, Frey & Chambers

By the 1940s, however, the modern style had become increasingly popular. And by the 1960s, very few new homes in Palm Springs were built in the traditional Spanish vernacular. Established architects with practices in Los Angeles, including Welton Becket (1902–1969), Conrad Buff III (1926–1989) and Donald C. Hensman (1924–2002), John Lautner (1911–1994) and A. Quincy Jones (1913–1979) were brought in to design second homes for their wealthy clients.

Some architects settled in the city, and adapted the International Style for desert living. Swiss-born Albert Frey (1903–1998), a disciple of Le Corbusier, moved from New York to Palm Springs in 1934 and teamed up with John Porter Clark (1905–1991) to form the most significant partnership in the desert, the first modern architects to live and practise in Palm Springs. The houses

they built for themselves, with flat roofs and wood frames sheathed in corrugated metal, put Palm Springs on the architectural map. Frey went on to produce over 200 residential, civic and commercial designs, including Palm Springs City Hall.

Located in the Coachella Valley in the Colorado desert, Palm Springs required a very different approach to building than other parts of the US. Temperatures rise to 125°F (52°C) in summer, with zero precipitation and humidity, and winds can be strong.

From a functional and aesthetic point of view, Frey's architecture was firmly rooted in the style of Le Corbusier. But he was also adept at using materials and designs that were appropriate to the desert. His designs were based on simple rectilinear compositions of planes that extended into the landscape, using standard industrial materials

which were readily available. They contributed to Palm Springs' reputation as a new frontier for modern architecture.

The year after Shulman had completed his photographs of Neutra's Grace Miller House, Frey built a house for himself on El Mirador, next to Via Donna – Frey House I, the first phase of which was completed in 1940. Although no longer standing, Shulman's photos of the house show Frey's new interest in extending wall planes into the landscape, an idea that he would explore further in his post-war projects. The tiny house, on a footprint of just 16x20 feet (4.9x6 metres) had a flat roof and corrugated aluminium-clad walls. Its design acknowledged the influence of Mies van der Rohe's German Pavilion for the 1929 International Exposition in Barcelona. The exterior aluminium cladding was painted a muted rose pink and

Frey House I Palm Springs, California. 1954
Architect: Albert Frey

Frey House I Palm Springs, California. 1954
Architect: Albert Frey

Frey House I Palm Springs, California. 1954
Architect: Albert Frey

Frey House I | Palm Springs, California. 1954

Frey House I Palm Springs, California. 1954

the interior slab cement walls were stained pink and green, reflecting the colours of the desert outside. Although there was just one interior room, the walls extending into the desert created exterior spaces, shaded by the overhanging roof.

Shulman recorded the evolution of the house for *House & Garden* magazine, as Frey developed and extended it in 1948 and 1953, and built a close working relationship with the architect. He also documented Frey's Palm Springs house for industrial designer Raymond Loewy (1893–1986) in 1947, and the North Shore Yacht Club on Salton Sea in 1960, an ode to the romance of the machine as was Frey's own first house.
Various schools for the Palm Springs Unified School District followed, as well as Palm Springs City Hall (1957), the Cree House II (1957), and the Valley Station of the Palm Springs Tramway (1964), from where visitors still soar from the valley floor up North America's sheerest mountain to San Jacinto Peak at 10,834 feet (3,302 metres).

Above: Albert Frey pictured outside Frey House I. 1954

Below: **Loewy House** Palm Springs, California. 1947
Architect: Clark & Frey

North Shore Yacht Club Salton Sea, California. 1960
Architect: Frey & Chambers

Driving east from Los Angeles along CA-111, you know when you have arrived in Palm Springs when you see the Tramway Gas Station – now a visitor centre – designed by Frey and Robson C. Chambers (1919–1999) in 1965. The dramatic roof structure, a hyperbolic paraboloid of steel I-beams with corrugated metal roofing, floats above the forecourt supported by just a few delicate steel tubular pillars. Shulman captured the structure in his inimitable style, the wedge-shaped roof erupting out of the landscape straight towards the camera.

After several years' searching for the perfect site, Frey built his second house (Frey House II) in 1964, 220 feet (67 metres) above Palm Springs, at the time the highest house in the city. The house, of simple form, is perfectly integrated with its site, wrapped around a natural

Above and Below:
Palm Springs Aerial Tramway Valley Station
Palm Springs, California. 1964
Architect: Albert Frey

Palm Springs Aerial Tramway Valley Station Palm Springs, California. 1964
Architect: Albert Frey

rock outcropping. A massive boulder has been incorporated into the house, dividing the bedroom from the living area and connecting the landscape to the interior in a dramatic expression of architectural context. The house is built on an east–west axis, and the resulting views across the Coachella Valley are spectacular. Shulman's photographs accentuate the setting, with many composed from the inside of the house looking directly east, down Tahquitz Canyon Way to the Santa Rosa Mountains beyond the sprawling city.

Shulman often photographed at dusk, during the time that Hollywood cinematographers would call the magic hour. While others are sipping ice-cold cocktails below in the Tennis Club bar or in the lounges of Palm Canyon Drive, from the parapet of Frey House II the viewer experiences an enchanted moment, frozen above the otherworldly spectacle.

Frey's arrival in the desert was followed by those of other talented and prolific architects. William F. Cody (1916–1978) settled there in 1945 and E. Stewart Williams (1909–2005) arrived in 1946, and with Frey and Clarke they developed Palm Springs' unique style of desert Modernism. Donald Wexler (1926–2015), who had previously worked for Neutra and is best known for his Steel Development Homes, followed in the early 1950s. Together, these architects affirmed Modernism's key propositions, with open floor plans and light structures, embracing the landscape. They provided exaggerated overhangs

Frey House II Palm Springs, California. 1965
Architect: Albert Frey

Frey House II Palm Springs, California. 1965
Architect: Albert Frey

Frey House II Palm Springs, California. 1965
Architect: Albert Frey

Frey House II Palm Springs, California. 1965
Architect: Albert Frey

Oasis Hotel, dining room Palm Springs, California. 1953
Architect: Williams, Williams & Williams

for additional shade, and thin steel beams afford strength without being obtrusive, allowing floor-to-ceiling windows and sliding doors, opening to outdoor pools and dramatic views of the mountains.

Palm Springs had been requisitioned as a military post and training ground during the Second World War. After the war, it was necessary to rehouse the military personnel who had worked there, as well as returning GIs who flocked to Palm Springs and the surrounding communities of Desert Hot Springs, Palm Desert and Rancho Mirage. A building boom ensued.

Development companies such as the Alexander Construction Company took full advantage, doubling the size of the city between 1955 and 1965. The company's association with architects Dan Palmer (1920–2007) and William Krisel (1924–2017) created a model for stylish, mass-produced, modern tract homes with clean lines

and simple elegance, complete with private swimming pools and twin palms. Modern architecture reflected the optimism and exuberance of the time and the availability of new materials, many of which had been developed during the war and were readily available in southern California. Air conditioning made year-round living possible in the desert, and new golfing communities and retirement homes sprang up in the valley.

Shulman made the desert his own, producing images that supported the mythology of the resort and made it all the more alluring for visitors and potential residents. He photographed projects for Neutra, A. Quincy Jones, Paul R. Williams (1894–1980), Frey, E. Stewart Williams, William F. Cody, Donald Wexler, Palmer and Krisel, John Lautner, Herbert Burns, Walter Wurdeman (1903–1949) and Welton Becket, William Leonard Pereira (1909–1985), Charles Luckman (1909–1999) and others. His Rolodex of architect clients working in the city was comprehensive, and he returned there time and again over a period of more than eight decades, to work, promote his clients and himself, to sign books and to hike in the canyons.

Coachella Valley Savings
Palm Springs, California. 1963
Architect: Williams & Williams

NEUTRA'S KAUFMANN HOUSE

In the shadow of the sandy-gold San Jacinto Mountains, the slopes of Palm Spring's Little Tuscany are strewn with huge boulders. Smoothed by the weather and softened by aromatic sage and thorny succulents, the brutal desert landscape provides an unlikely context for one of architecture's great experiments. Here Neutra built a winter house for Pittsburgh department store owner Edgar J. Kaufmann (1885–1955), which is arguably one of the most important examples of International Style architecture in the US.

The Kaufmann House, completed in 1946, glitters like ice in this desert landscape, at once complementing it and presiding over it. Its flat roof planes are edged with silver, which glint in the unyielding sun and hover over transparent walls of glass. It is a sculptural object whose geometric forms contrast dramatically with the desert around it. And yet it reaches out into the landscape, drawing it into its cool interior.

Kaufmann was no stranger to International Style Modernism. He had commissioned Frank Lloyd Wright to build Fallingwater in southwestern Pennsylvania, which the AIA named "the best all-time work of American architecture." For his desert commission, however, Kaufmann passed over Wright's proposal, perhaps inspired by his visit to Neutra's Miller House. At $300,000, the budget for the 3,800-square foot (353-square metre) Kaufmann House was exorbitant.

Shulman canonised the Kaufmann House, making over 50 photographs of the residence, and helped to make it an architectural icon. Published in *Architectural Forum* and *Life* magazine in August 1949, the best-known image shows the house at dusk, its geometric architectural forms perfectly juxtaposed against a backdrop of dissolving mountains. Liliane Kaufmann reclines by the pool, seemingly oblivious to the onset of night. Along with Shulman's night-time image of CHS#22 in Los

Kaufmann House Palm Springs, California. 1949
Architect: Richard Neutra

Kaufmann House Palm Springs, California. 1949
Architect: Richard Neutra

Angeles, this photograph is among his most recognised works of art.

Shulman described the setting:

"I had been doing photographs with Neutra at the house, and towards evening, as the sun was setting, I noticed, looking out to the eastern desert, there was a beautiful glow in the sky, and I said to Mr Neutra, 'Just a moment. I want to go outside and look at the house from the eastern side of the property.' I looked at the house and I thought, 'My God! Look at the twilight developing, and look at the mountains, and the scene which was being created by the changing light!' So I quickly ran into the house, against the will of Neutra, because Neutra was insistent that we continue working, because he wanted to do more interiors in the house. So I said, 'No, Richard, we can't do that. That sky is beautiful, the mountains are beautiful, and the light glowing inside, the exposure values are just right.'

So I ran out with my camera and my film bag, and I set up the camera, and out of this came this photograph. And I had a shutter which didn't have to be cocked. You can open and close this shutter at will, expose two or three seconds at a time, and then run into the house and turn on lights, turn off lights, and built, kept, like building blocks, kept building my exposure for this scene. And out of this came this photograph. Now the point I'm making is I didn't know what I was doing. All I knew was it was a beautiful thing, and I was going to try to capture the elements of this design and the mood of the mountains, the twilight, the magic. It turns out this is one of the two most widely published architectural photographs in the world." [lxvi]

Kaufmann House Palm Springs, California. 1949
Architect: Richard Neutra

POSTMODERNISM
'LESS IS A BORE'

By the 1970s, Modernism had faded from fashion. The formalism of the International Style was replaced by the whimsy of postmodernism with wit, ornament and stylistic reference embellishing the new architectural forms. Architect Robert Venturi (1925–2018), at the forefront of the postmodern architectural movement, adapted Mies van der Rohe's maxim "less is more" to 'less is a bore', and architects rediscovered the expressive and symbolic elements of the past.

Shulman's order book gradually declined. He condemned postmodernism for being less concerned with designing spaces for living and more with superficial and frivolous façades. He did not feel that he could photograph the projects that he was offered with integrity, finding postmodernist architecture unappealing, even abhorrent.

He was also at retirement age, and a younger generation of architectural photographers, including the British-born Tim Street-Porter and Australian-born Grant Mudford (1944–), were assuming his mantle in Los Angeles. Partly as a result, Shulman officially retired in 1989.

He was never completely out of the limelight, however. In the same year, the Museum of Contemporary Art in Los Angeles presented a landmark exhibition, 'Blueprints for Modern Living: History and Legacy of the Case Study Houses'. The exhibition, curated by Elizabeth A.T. Smith, who also edited the accompanying book,[lxvii] introduced the Case Study programme to a new generation of architects and the wider public, which generated renewed interest in International Style architecture in the process. The exhibition and book drew heavily on Shulman's photographic archive and featured a full-scale model of CSH#22.

Piazza d'Italia New Orleans. 2006
Architect: Charles Moore
Photographer: Christina Holland

SHULMAN THE CAMPAIGNER
PRESERVATION AND ENVIRONMENT

Although the demolition of Irving Gill's (1870–1936) Walter L. Dodge House (950 N. Kings Rd., West Hollywood, California, completed 1916) galvanised Los Angeles' architectural preservation movement as early as 1970, it was not until 1984 that the Los Angeles Conservancy was to form a Fifties Task Force, later to be renamed the Modern Committee (ModCom). The inspiration was the demolition for redevelopment of Ships Coffee Shop and Chicken Galley at Westwood and Glendon (a fine example of Googie architecture) on September 21st the same year, as well as other important midcentury modern landmarks.

Interest in International Style architecture continued to be rekindled in the 1990s and 2000s,

driven in large part by the huge popularity and ubiquity of Julius Shulman's photographs, which helped to drive a revival in Modernist architecture and interior design. With the 2000 publication of *Modernism Rediscovered*,[lxviii] publisher Benedikt Taschen delved deep into Shulman's archives to reveal the masterpieces of midcentury modern architecture. With text by Pierluigi Serraino and Julius Shulman, the book brought new appreciation for Shulman's photographic genius and for the nearly 300 residences represented.

In Palm Springs, as elsewhere, the midcentury modern style had fallen out of favour by the 1970s and the recession of 1973–1975 forced many people with second homes in the desert to sell up. Twenty-five years

Beth Edwards Harris and Julius Shulman discussing the Kaufmann House

of deterioration followed, with many iconic buildings being demolished, badly remodelled or altered beyond recognition. A photograph of Palm Springs Tramway Gas Station made in 1997 by Canadian photographer Robert Polidori (1951–) shows it destitute and abandoned. That year, a developer had proposed a $40m entertainment centre that would have required the demolition of the historic structure. Thanks to preservation advocacy efforts, Palm Springs City Council voted to save the station and restore it as the Palm Springs Visitors Center. This marked a turning point in the preservation of the desert Modernism of Palm Springs. The building was listed on the National Register of Historic Places in 2015.

The Kaufmann House suffered a similar fate: when Edgar Kaufmann died in 1955, the house remained empty for several years before being sold to a series of owners, including singer Barry Manilow and the owner of the San Diego Chargers football team, Eugene V. Klein. The house was renovated and altered over the following decades, with patios enclosed, floral wallpaper hung on the walls and the addition of a media room. In 1992 architectural historian Beth Edwards Harris rediscovered it and with her husband Brent Harris commissioned Los Angeles architectural firm Marmol Radziner to restore it to its authentic state. The architect's drawings were no longer available and Neutra had died in 1970, so the Harrises and their architects relied heavily on Shulman's photographs, taken nearly half a century before, to give clues as to the original design.

Neutra had predicted the importance of Shulman's photographs in preserving his architecture: "*His work will survive me. Film is stronger and good glossy prints are easier to ship

than brute concrete, stainless steel, or even ideas.*" [lxix] Shulman's art, however, has ensured that Neutra's architecture will survive, if only in a modified form.

Leo Marmol and Ron Radziner tracked down firms that could replicate elements no longer in production and consulted octogenarian contractor 'Red' Fordyce Marsh, who had built some 20 Neutra houses. They convinced a quarry in Utah to reopen and cut new sandstone in the original pink-buff

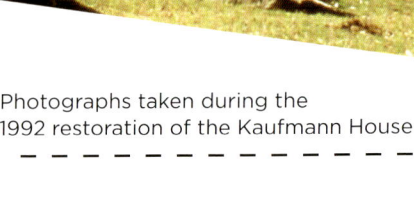

Photographs taken during the 1992 restoration of the Kaufmann House

Case Study House #20 Altadena, California. 1958

Kaufmann House (restored) Palm Springs, California. 1998
Architect: Richard Neutra

Kaufmann House (restored) Palm Springs, California. 1998
Architect: Richard Neutra
Restoration architect: Marmol Radziner

Case Study House #21 Los Angeles, California. 1958
Architect: Pierre Koenig

hue to replace sections that had been removed or damaged, and meticulously reproduced other components. Window frames, door furniture, light fittings and cabinetry were restored or replicated, all with the aid of Shulman's photographic archive.

After the restoration was complete, Shulman returned to re-photograph the house and found it exactly as he remembered it from 1947. The AIA awarded Marmol Radziner the National Honor Award in 2000, setting the gold standard for restoration of modern architecture. The house was sold at auction for $15m. Auction firm Christie's marketed the house as a work of art, listing it as part of a post-war and contemporary art evening sale in May 2008. This followed a precedent for selling real estate as art set by the 2003 sale of Mies van der Rohe's Farnsworth House (built 1951). Needless to say, the Christie's catalogue for the sale was generously illustrated with Shulman photographs.

The restoration sparked a renewed energy for preserving and restoring the masterworks of the midcentury modern period. Marmol and Radziner went on to restore Neutra's Brown House in Bel Air (built 1955, restored 1998); Frey's Loewy House in Palm Springs (built 1947, restored 2000); Buff, Straub & Hensman's Katleman Residence in Beverly Hills (built 1963,

restored 2000); Schindler's Elliot House in Los Angeles (built 1930, restored 2001); and Neutra's CSH#20 Stuart Bailey House (built 1948, restored 2003). These were followed by John Lautner's Garcia House in Los Angeles (built 1962, restored 2005); Cliff May's Experimental Ranch in Los Angeles (built 1952, restored 2007); and E. Stewart Williams' Santa Fe Federal Savings and Loan building in Palm Springs (built 1960, restored 2014), which the Palm Springs Art Museum acquired in 2011 to house architecture and design exhibitions and programs. Many of these important reconstructions relied on Shulman's photographs to guide the restoration architects.

The restoration of Pierre Koenig's CSH#21 Walter Bailey House (1958) can also be closely linked to the abiding power of Shulman's photographs. In 1997 film producer Dan Cracchiolo, a fan of Julius Shulman's photography, bought the house for $1.5m. The house had gone through many alterations over the years, with the original kitchen having been demolished and other changes that wreaked havoc with Koenig's initial design. Cracchiolo employed Koenig himself to restore the house to its original glory, and even commissioned replicas of the Formica entry cabinet and Naugahyde-covered sofa shown in Shulman's original photographs. The result was a sympathetic and authentic restoration, which made just a few concessions to the requirements of 1990s living.

With the success of *Modernism Rediscovered*, Shulman came out of retirement in 2000 and joined forces with German-born photographer Juergen Nogai (1953–). Shulman was once more in demand to photograph not only the classics of midcentury modern architecture, but also new architecture inspired by the clean, simple lines and central ideology of the International Style. Some 48 years after he had first photographed CSH#21, in 2006 the 96-year-old Julius Shulman was invited back to photograph the house with Nogai for the catalogue of its sale by auction. The resulting photographs are as fresh and evocative as any of Shulman's earlier works, and show his ability to endure and remain relevant.

The importance of Julius Shulman's photographs in this process should not be underestimated. One of the keys to Shulman's success as a businessman was the impeccable way that he – and his daughter Judy Shulman McKee – had maintained his archival reference system. Cavalcades of dark green and gunmetal-grey steel filing cabinets were arranged in his studio, containing negatives dating back to his schooldays, test prints and transparencies.

They also held thousands of 3x5-inch index cards, on which every project was allocated a job number and cross-referenced by architect, date and print details. Some cards also list the client, and in a few cases, the publications in which the images were published. Architects and house owners alike foraged through these archives for

inspiration and clues to the intentions of the original architects. Shulman was a willing accomplice in this process, welcoming architects, photographers, students, home

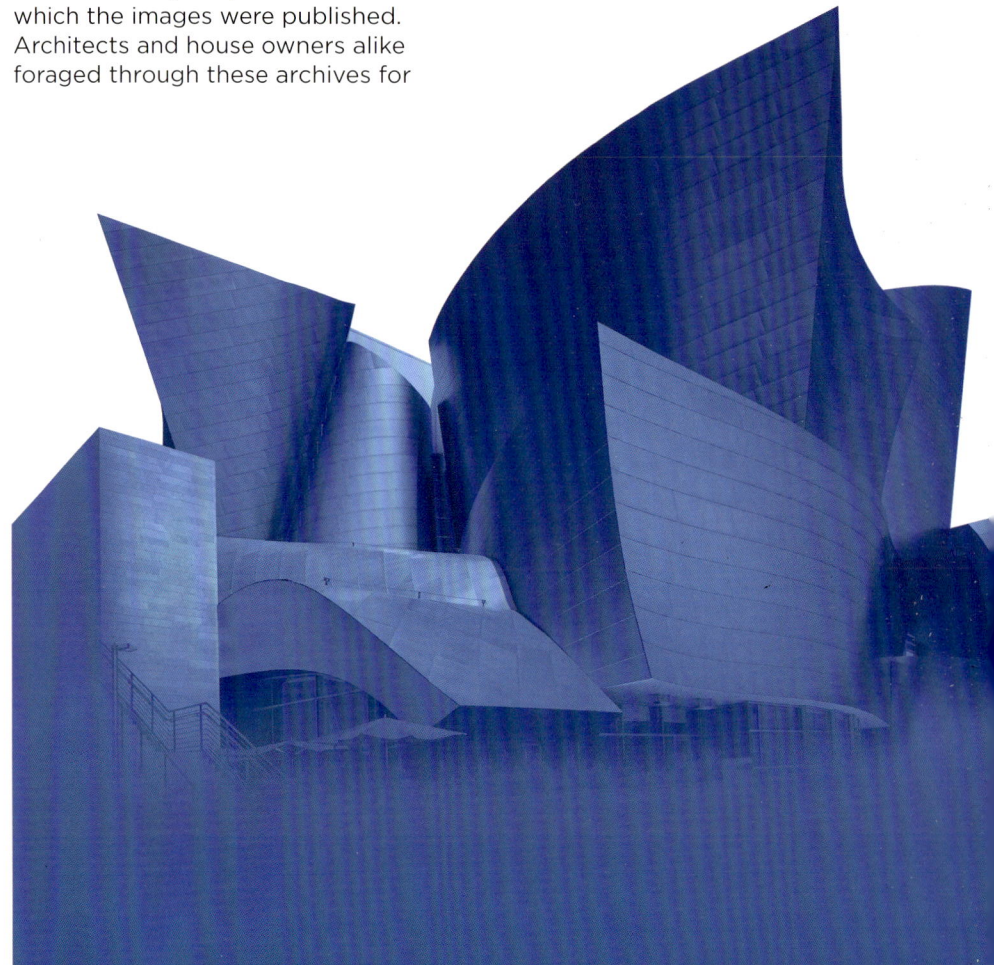

Walt Disney Concert Hall Los Angeles, California. 2004 👁
Architect: Frank Gehry

Segel House Malibu, California. 1980
Architect: John Lautner

Garcia House Los Angeles, California. 1980
Architect: John Lautner

The Getty Center Los Angeles, California. 1998
Architect: Richard Meier

owners, journalists, filmmakers and architectural enthusiasts from around the world into his Laurel Canyon studio. He would sit cheerfully in his Arne Jacobsen Egg Chair, or behind his desk, cluttered with prints and papers, his red telephone – always answered by Shulman himself – ringing continuously.

Shulman and Nogai went on to re-photograph many of the houses that Shulman had worked on between the 1940s and 1960s. Their diaries also filled up with commissions to photograph new works compatible with Shulman's lofty architectural standards. The partners made stunning new images of Abraham Zabludovsky's Children's Museum in Mexico, Frank Gehry's (1929–) Walt Disney Concert Hall and Richard Meier's (1934–) Getty Center. They also photographed new residential spaces by emerging architects Jeffrey Eyster (1970–), Don Boss, Zoltan Pali (1960–), William Francis Cody (1916–1978), Steven Ehrlich (1946–) and many others. Much of the new work was in colour, photographed using Shulman's 4x5-inch plate film camera, with vibrant digital prints adding a new dimension to his repertoire.

The historical and academic importance of Shulman's work was recognised in 2005 when the Getty Research Institute acquired his archive of some 260,000 prints, negatives and transparencies, to be preserved, digitised and catalogued for future generations. The collection represents a unique chronicle of West Coast architecture from 1936, as well as of industrial design and significant buildings elsewhere in the US, South America, Asia and Europe. In October 2005, the Getty Research Institute mounted an exhibition, 'Julius Shulman: Modernity and the Metropolis', to coincide with his 95th birthday celebrations.

Even at that age, Shulman used the occasion to campaign for the preservation of the city that had been his home for 85 years. During an interview with Wim de Wit, at

the time, head of the Department of Architecture and Contemporary Art at the Getty Research Institute, Shulman talked of his love of nature and for Los Angeles, and how the city that he knew as a younger man had become an ugly sprawl with no intelligent city plan. Shulman turned his head to view a slide of a smoggy tangle of houses and highways; *"How would you like to live in that pile of junk?"* he asked.[lxx]

Rarely modest about his achievements, he commented, "I sell more architecture than the architects" and *"Often people were more impressed with my photographs than with the houses*

themselves.' [lxxi] But to the end of his life, Shulman remained Modernism's most eloquent ambassador.

In a 2011 exhibition at Los Angeles County Museum of Art, the entire living room from the Eames House (CSH#8) was meticulously removed and reassembled in a replica of the house while the original house was being restored. The exhibition claimed to be "the first major study of California midcentury modern design", examining California's "role in shaping the material culture of the entire country". Shulman's photographs inevitably played an important role in the exhibition and catalogue.[lxxii]

Case Study House #8 Pacific Palisades, California. 1950
Architect: Charles & Ray Eames

Crystal Cathedral Welcoming Center Garden Grove, California. 2006 👁
Architect: Richard Meier

Hill House Pacific Palisades, California. 2004 👁
Architect: Johnston Marklee & Associates

Glass House New Canaan, Connecticut. 2006 👁
Architect: Philip Johnson

Children's Museum Villa Hermosa, Mexico. 2005 👁

Shulman's extraordinary energy, optimism, sense of humour and passion for architecture continued to keep city councils and developers on their toes and helped to build awareness of the hidden treasures to be rediscovered in cities everywhere. But even when protection seemed assured by preservation orders enforced by local city councils, fine examples continued to be lost. In April 2002, an unscrupulous developer demolished Neutra's Maslon House at the Tamarisk Country Club near Palm Springs, which Shulman had photographed in 1963. And in September 2014 the Palm Springs Spa Resort hotel was torn down, taking with it the classic colonnaded entrance that Donald Wexler had designed (and Shulman had photographed) in 1959. To the end of his life, Shulman strove to bring the plight of such important structures to the public's attention.

He was not just concerned with the protection of the architectural classics, however. Shulman was a vocal advocate for controlling the expansion of Los Angeles and other cities around the US, and protecting the environment from unethical or ill-informed speculators. As developers ripped out thousands of square miles of orange groves to build ever more tract houses and apartment buildings, and a tangle of freeways choked Los Angeles with smog, Shulman became disillusioned with what was happening to his city.

Even as early as 1964 he had started a programme called 'Project: Environment USA', collaborating with architects, designers and artists. The organisation developed new ideas about how architects and developers could relate their work to good environmental practice. The project toured for a decade throughout the U.S. with selections from 150 30x40-inch enlargements that Shulman had made specially.

Shulman's love of the city and the magnificent southern California landscape in which he had grown up inspired him to campaign tirelessly for environmental issues for the rest of his life. "*History is strange.*

Here, it becomes mystical," Julius Shulman said of his beloved Los Angeles. He knew that some of his causes would take much of his life to be accepted by the world at large, but Shulman, philosophical as ever, was not in a hurry: "*Why hurry?*" he asked. "*The secret of being freelance is being free. Then you can toss the lance and have the freedom to go wherever it lands. There are very few things in the world that are so important that they can't wait.*" [lxxiii]

"*I tell students, 'Don't take life too seriously – don't plan nothing nohow.' But I have always observed and respected my destiny. That's the only way I can describe it. It was meant to be.*" [lxxiv]

Palm Springs Spa Palm Springs, California. 1961
Architect: Architect: William Cody in association with Philip Koenig, Wexler and Harrison.

SHULMAN THE EDUCATOR

From early in his career, Shulman was involved in education. He was concerned about the shortage of commercial photographers in the US, particularly with a focus on architectural photography. As construction boomed after the Second World War, Shulman recognised that there was a need for more architectural photographers, and set about organising workshops with the AIA and schools of architecture to show his techniques to a new generation of photographers, encouraging collaborative work with architects to forge stronger bonds between the professions. By the 1960s, Shulman was extending this educational work to writing. He published *Photographing Architecture and Interiors* in 1962,[lxxv] followed by *The Photography of Architecture and Design* in 1977.[lxxvi]

In a perfect blending of his photographic and educational interest with his love of nature and the great outdoors, Shulman accepted an invitation in 1983 from the great landscape photographer, Ansel Adams, to run a workshop at Yosemite National Park on 'The Architecture of Nature', to help photographers understand the relationship between nature and architecture.

Shulman was always generous with his knowledge, and for decades conducted seminars in photography at the University of Southern California, UCLA and other universities. In 2005, Shulman founded the Julius Shulman Institute at Woodbury University in Burbank, CA, to promote understanding and appreciation of the photography of the built environment. In the same year, the university awarded Shulman an honorary doctorate of architecture.

Below right: Julius Shulman accepts his honorary doctorate in 2005

Below: Shulman mentoring students

SHULMAN THE ARTIST

In the film *Visual Acoustics: The Modernism of Julius Shulman*, artist Ed Ruscha (1937–) comments, *"Shulman's pictures have this base of romance to them. His work represents a certain ideal that happened years ago."* Even though a number of architectural photographers before Shulman had achieved a degree of recognition for their craft, architectural photography was not considered to be a serious art form until at least the 1940s.

By the end of the Second World War, art photographers had already achieved celebrity status for their work, shared widely in consumer magazines. This tended not to be true for commercial architectural photographers. After the war, however, modern architecture in the US and the United Kingdom became a metaphor for a better life, and popular magazines reflected this. Architectural photographers – such as F.S. Lincoln, Fred R. Dapprich and Roger Sturtevant in the US; and British photographers Herbert Felton (1888-1968), John Havinden (1908-1987) and Mark Oliver Dell (1883-1959) and his partner at *The*

Architectural Review, H.L.Wainwright – developed a photographic method which embraced modern architecture and reflected its ideals. According to Calcagno and Nikolova (2015), *"Modelled after American fashion photography, the new architectural photography created seductive statements about a comfortable lifestyle and the architecture through which it could be achieved."* [lxxvii]

Although the purpose of most of Shulman's photographs was originally commercial, they have gained cultural significance. Transcending their original function, they are now considered important works of art. They reflect a glittering world, populated by beautiful, successful people, framed by the pure, simple lines of modern architecture and untethered landscape. The aspirations of Americans hoping and striving for a better life are crystalised in his exquisite prints, which embody the Californian dream.

Julius, of course, went one step further: *"I think the photographer can go beyond the artist. I can create a summation of the total image of what was in the architect's mind, the physical aspects of the structure, and, of course, the spirit."* [lxxviii] Although he set out as a journeyman commercial photographer, Shulman has become widely regarded as a significant artist, documenting midcentury US life and landscape, and matching the accomplishments of Adams, Ruscha, and David Hockney. Shulman's images are also widely exhibited as art and sold in art galleries and auctions around the world.

Among his many accolades, in 1969 the AIA awarded Shulman the Gold Medal for Architectural Photography and in 1980 inducted him as an honorary member. In 1998 the International Center of Photography gave him a Lifetime Achievement Award; in 2003 *Interior Design* magazine inducted him into the Hall of Fame; in 2004 he was Honouree for Outstanding Achievement in

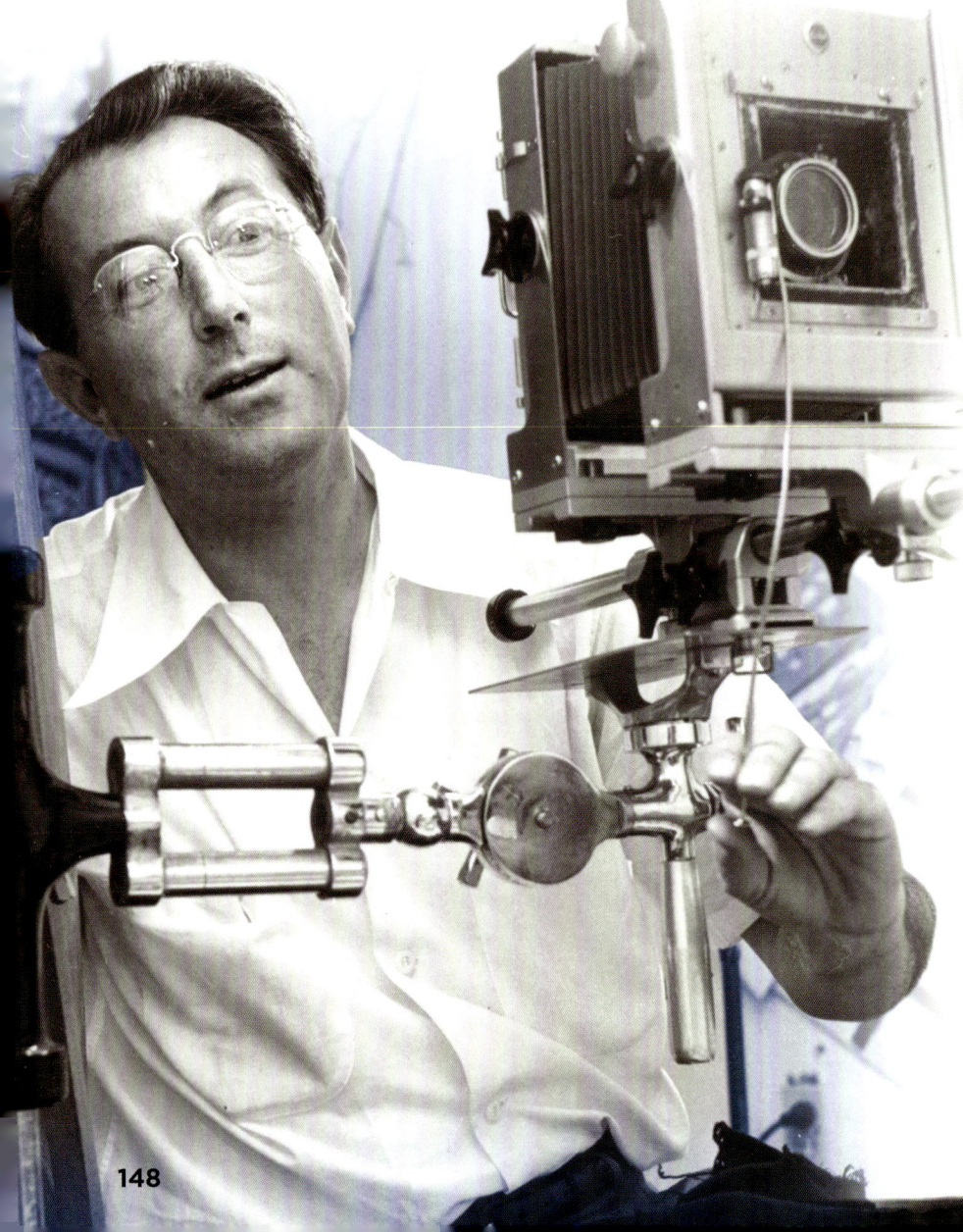

Architecture Photography at the Lucie Awards; and in 2006 he was awarded a Golden Palm Star on the Palm Springs Walk of Stars.

Shulman maintained his energy and remained an evangelist for southern California, environmental issues, education and the preservation of the architecture that he loved until his death on 15 July 2009, aged 98. Shulman's first wife, Emma, died in 1973. In 1976, he married Olga, who died in 1999. His daughter Judy and grandson Timothy live in Santa Barbara.

Julius Shulman's house at 7875 Woodrow Wilson Drive in the Hollywood Hills was sold in 2010 for $2.25m, with 0.87 acres (0.35 hectares) of the original lot. It has since been renovated by Los Angeles-based firm Lorcan O'Herlihy Architects (LOHA). Shulman's semi-detached office studio has been turned into a guest suite. ●

Life is good. Life can be beautiful. What more can I ask? [lxxix]

Julius Shulman

Case Study House #22 (Stahl House) Los Angeles, California. 1960
Architect: Pierre Koenig

Chemosphere Los Angeles, California. 1961
Architect: John Lautner

Chuey House Los Angeles, California. 1960
Architect: Richard Neutra

Singleton House Los Angeles, California. 1960
Architect: Richard Neutra

Duffield's Lincoln-Mercury Showroom Long Beach, California. 1963
Architect: Killingsworth, Brady & Smith

Los Angeles Department of Water and Power Los Angeles, California. 1966
Architect: A.C. Martin & Associates

Los Angeles by Night Los Angeles, California. 1956

Los Angeles by Night Los Angeles, California. 1956

REFERENCES

Weston, Edward and Newhall, Nancy (1973) 'The Daybooks of Edward Weston', *New York: Aperture*

Bayley, Stephen (2014) 'The camera always lies', *The Spectator*, September:
www.spectator.co.uk/2014/09/i-saw-my-city-through-a-lens-we-all-do/

Betjeman, John (1938) *An Oxford University Chest*, London: John Miles

Calcagno, Gianfranco and Nikolova, Irina (2015) 'History of Architectural Photography and its Unique Challenges', DPTips Central:
www.dptips-central.com/architectural-photography.html

Campany, David (2014) 'Architecture as Photography: document, publicity, commentary, art':
http://davidcampany.com/architecture-as-photography-document-publicity-commentary/

Cartier-Bresson, Henri (1952) *The Decisive Moment (Images à la Sauvette)*, New York: Simon and Schuster in collaboration with Editions Verve, Paris

Ciampaglia, Dante A. (2015) 'Review: Pedro E. Guerrero: A Photographer's Journey, American Masters', *Architectural Record*, 22 September 2015:
http://archrecord.construction.com/news/2015/09/150922-Review-American-Masters-8212-Pedro-E-Guerrero-A-Photographer8217s-Journey.asp

Crosse, John (2009) Southern California Architectural History, 27 December:
https://socalarchhistory.blogspot.co.uk/2009_12_01_archive.html

Ford, James and Morrow Ford, Katherine (1946) *The Modern House in America*, New York: Architectural Book Publishers

Goldberger, Paul (1989) 'Architecture; When Modernism Kissed The Land of Golden Dreams', *The New York Times*, 10 December:
www.nytimes.com/1989/12/10/arts/architecture-when-modernism-kissed-the-land-of-golden-dreams.html?pagewanted=all

Hitchcock, Henry-Russell (1936) 'The Architecture of H.H. Richardson and His Times' New York: Museum of Modern Art

Hitchcock, Henry-Russell and Johnson, Philip (1932) *The International Style: Architecture Since 1922*, New York: W.W. Norton

Icon Photography School (2011) '154 Incredible Photography Quotes': **https://photographyicon.com/quotes/**

International Centre of Photography (n.d.) 'Julius Shulman: Biography':
www.icp.org/browse/archive/constituents/julius-Shulman?all/all/all/all/0

Jencks, Charles (2013) 'Architecture Becomes Music', *The Architectural Review*, 6 May:
www.architectural-review.com/rethink/viewpoints/architecture-becomes-music/8647050.fullarticle

Kaplan, Wendy (2011) *California Design, 1930–1965: 'Living in a Modern Way'*, Cambridge, MA: MIT Press

Katzenstein, Bill (2008) 'History of Architectural Photography: Book Review', *Shutter Release*, August:
www.iconicphoto.com/pdf/history_book_review_0808.pdf

Kristal, Marc (2015) 'Modern Spirit: Remembering Julius Shulman', *The Line*, 22 June:
www.theline.com/vol/chapter/remembering_julius_Shulman

Kristal, Marc (2009) 'True Hollywood Story', *Dwell* magazine, 16 July:
www.dwell.com/profiles/article/true-hollywood-story

Kaufman, Mervyn D. (1969) *Father of Skyscrapers: A Biography of Louis Sullivan*, Boston, MA: Little, Brown and Company

Lamprecht, Barbara (2000) *Neutra, Complete Works*, Cologne and New York: Taschen

Le Corbusier (1924) *Vers Une Architecture*, Paris: G. Crès et Cie

Loos, Adolph (1908) 'Ornament and Crime', lecture, first published in *Cahiers d'aujourd'hui* (issue 5 of 1910)

MacCarthy, Fiona (2006) 'The Fiery Stimulator', *Guardian*, 18 March:
www.theguardian.com/artanddesign/2006/mar/18/art.modernism

Melton, Mary (2009) 'Lens Master', *Los Angeles Times*, 1 January 2009:
www.lamag.com/longform/lens-master1/

Miles Gardiner, Michelle (2005) 'Julius Shulman: Modernity and the Metropolis at the Getty', *Splash Magazines*:
http://www.lasplash.com/publish/cat_index_art_and_books/Julius_Shulman_Modernity_and_the_Metropolis.php

Moholy-Nagy, László (1922) 'Constructivism and the proletariat' ['Konstruktivismus und Proletariat'], *MA*, May, excerpts reprinted in Sibyl Moholy-Nagy (1950) *Experiment in Totality*, New York: Harper & Brothers, p. 19

Moholy-Nagy, László and Hoffmann, Daphne M. (1932) *The New Vision, from Material to Architecture*, New York: Brewer, Warren & Putnam, Inc.

Nakano, Craig (2005) 'A Photographic Memory', *Los Angeles Times*, 3 March:
http://articles.latimes.com/2005/mar/03/home/hm-Shulman3

Quddus, Sadia (2014) 'The Berlage Archive: Julius Shulman (2000)', *Arch Daily*, 11 November:
www.archdaily.com/566014/the-berlage-archive-julius-Shulman-2000/

Rattenbury, K. (2002) *Iconic Pictures. This is not Media Architecture*, London and New York: Routledge

Rikala de Noreiga, Taina (2010) Interview with Julius Shulman (1990), 19 June:
www.americansuburbx.com/2010/06/interview-interview-with-julius-Shulman-1990.html

Rockwood, Camilla (2007) *Chambers Biographical Dictionary*, London: Chambers Harrap

Shulman, Julius (1977) *The Photography of Architecture and Design: Photographing Buildings, Interiors and the Visual Arts*, London: Architectural Press

Shulman, Julius; Gössel, Peter; and O'Gehry, Frank (1998) *Architecture and Its Photography*, Cologne and New York: Taschen

Shulman, Julius and Harris, Mark Edward (2000) *Julius Shulman: Photographing Architecture and Interiors*, Los Angeles: Balcony Press

Shulman, Julius (1962) *Photographing Architecture and Interiors*, New York: Whitney Library of Design

Shulman, Julius and Serraino, Pierluigi (2000) *Modernism Rediscovered*, Cologne: Taschen

Smith, Elizabeth and McCoy, Esther (1989) *Blueprints for Modern Living: History and Legacy of The Case Study Houses*, Cambridge, MA: MIT Press

Spence, Amanda (2015) 'Where have all the people gone?', *The Architects' Journal*, 19 September:
www.architectsjournal.co.uk/culture/where-have-all-the-people-gone/8689031.article

Sullivan, Louis (1924) *Autobiography of an Idea*, New York City: Press of the American Institute of Architects

Teicholz, Tom (2007) 'Picturing LA (Julius Shulman)', *Tommywood,* 18 November:
http://tommywood.com/picturing-la-julius-Shulman/

Time (2016) 'Case Study House No. 22, Los Angeles – 1960, Julius Shulman':
http://100photos.time.com/photos/julius-shulman-case-study-house-22

Walker, Alissa (1999) *A Tribute to Architecture's Best Photographer, Julius Shulman*, Fast Company, 21 July:
www.fastcompany.com/1313946/tribute-architectures-best-photographer-julius-Shulman

Woods, Mary N. (2009) *Beyond the Architect's Eye: Photographs and the American Built Environment*, Philadelphia, PA: University of Pennsylvania Press

Wright, Frank Lloyd (1911) *Ausgeführte Bauten und Entwürfe von Frank Lloyd Wright*, Berlin: Ernst Wasmuth

FURTHER READING

Atget, Eugène, and Abbott, Berenice (1964) *The World of Atget*, New York: Horizon Press

Atget, Eugène; MacOrlan, Pierre; Abbott, Berenice and Jonquières, Henri (1930) *Atget: Photographe de Paris*, New York: E. Weyhe

Becher, Bernhard and Hilla (1970) *Anonyme Skulpturen: Eine Typologie technischer Bauten*, Düsseldorf: Art Press Verlag

Benjamin, Walter (2005) *A Little History of Photography (1931), Selected Writings: 1931–1934*, Michael W. Jennings (ed.), tr. Rodney Livingstone and others, Cambridge, MA: Belknap Press of Harvard University Press

Colomina, Beatriz (1996) *Privacy and Publicity: Modern Architecture as Mass Media*, Cambridge, MA: MIT Press

Cygelman, Adèle, (1999) *Palm Springs Modern: Houses in the California Desert*, New York: Rizzoli International Publications

Dailey, Victoria, Shivers, Natalie and Dawson, Michael (2003) *LA's Early Moderns: Art / Architecture / Photography*, Los Angeles: Balcony Press

Darling, Michael; Helfrich, Kurt G. F; Smith, Elizabeth; Sweeney, Robert; Wilson, Richard Guy [contributors] (2001) *The Architecture of R.M. Schindler*, The Museum of Contemporary Art, Los Angeles, New York: Harry N. Abrams

Elwall, R. (2004) *Building with Light. The International History of Architectural Photography*, London: Merrell

Fairley, Alastair (2006) *De La Warr Pavilion: The Modernist Masterpiece*, London: Merrell

Golub, Jennifer (1999) *Albert Frey / Houses 1 + 2*, New York: Princeton Architectural Press

Harris, Michael (2001) *Professional Architectural Photography*, London: Focal Press

Higgott, Andrew and Wray, Timothy (2012) *Camera Constructs: Photography, Architecture and The Modern City*, Abingdon-on-Thames: Routledge

Ince, Catherine and Johnson, Lotte (2015) *The World of Charles and Ray Eames*, London: Thames and Hudson

Jackson, Lesley, (1994) *Contemporary: Architecture and Interiors of the 1950s*, London: Phaidon Press Ltd

Kabilan, S. (2012) *Impact of Photography on Modern Architecture*, 4th Yr Sec 'A' dissertation, School of Planning and Architecture, New Delhi: **https://issuu.com/kabi1990/docs/impact_of_photography_on_modern_architecture**

Leet, Stephen (2004) *Richard Neutra's Miller House*, New York: Princeton Architectural Press

Maraca, Marco (ed.) (2015) *The Desert Modernists: The Architects Who Envisioned Midcentury Modern Palm Springs*, Palm Springs, CA: Modernism Week and Desert Publications Inc.

McGrath, Norman (2011) *Architectural Photography: Professional Techniques for Shooting Interior and Exterior Spaces*, London: Amphoto Books

Melton, Mary (2009) 'Lens Master', *Los Angeles Times*, 1 January 2009: **www.lamag.com/longform/lens-master1/**

Menrad, Chris and Creighton, Heidi (2016) *William Krisel's Palm Springs: The Language of Modernism*, Layton, UT: Gibbs Smith

Moholy-Nagy, László (1969) *The Future of the Photographic Process* (Malerei, Fotografie, Film, 1925), reprinted in English, Cambridge, MA: MIT Press

Newhall, Nancy (ed.) (1971), *Edward Weston: The Flame of Recognition*, New York, Aperture

Picton, Tom (1979) 'The Craven Image, or The Apotheosis of the Architectural Photograph', *The Architects' Journal*, 25 July

Rappaport, Nina and Stoller, Erica (2012) *Ezra Stoller, Photographer*, New Haven, CT: Yale University Press

Redstone, Elias; Gadanho, Pedro; Bush, Kate (2014) *Shooting Space: Architecture in Contemporary Photography*, London: Phaidon Press

Robinson, Cervin and Herschman, Joel (2001) *Architecture Transformed: A History of Photography of Buildings from 1893 to the Present*, Cambridge, MA: MIT Press

Rosa, Joseph (1999) *Albert Frey, Architect*, New York: Princeton Architectural Press

Rosa, Joseph (1994) *A Constructed View: The Architectural Photography of Julius Shulman*, New York: Rizzoli International Publications

Rothenstein, Michael (1946) 'Colour and Modern Architecture, or "The Photographic Eye"', *The Architectural Review*, vol. XLIV, May

Saunders, William S. (1990) *Modern Architecture: Photographs by Ezra Stoller*, New York: Harry N. Abram

Schirmböck, Thomas (2011) *Julius Shulman: The Last Decade. Photographs by Julius Shulman / Jürgen Nogai*, Heidelberg : Kehrer Verlag

Scully, Vincent (1961) *Modern Architecture, The Architecture of Democracy*, New York: George Braziller

Shore, Stephen (2008) 'Photography and Architecture (1997)', in Christy Lange, Stephen Shore, Michael Fried and Joel Sternfeld, *Stephen Shore*, New York: Phaidon Press

Smith, Elizabeth (2002) *Case Study Houses: The Complete CSH Program, 1945-1966*, Cologne: Taschen

Snibbe, Patricia and Snibbe, Richard (1999) *The New Modernist in World Architecture*, New York: McGraw-Hill

Stern, Michael and Hess, Alan (2008) *Julius Shulman: Palm Springs*, New York: Rizzoli International Publications

Stoller, Ezra (1999) *The Yale Art + Architecture Building*, New York: Building Blocks (an imprint of Princeton Architectural Press)

Street-Porter, Tim and Keaton, Diane (2006) *Los Angeles*, New York: Rizzoli

Temko, Allan, (1962) *Eero Saarinen [Makers Of Contemporary Architecture]*, New York: G. Braziller

Weiner, Stewart (Editor) (2015) *The Desert Modernists: The Architects Who Envisioned Midcentury Modern Palm Springs*, Palm Springs: Modernism Week

Weston, Richard (1996) *Modernism*, London: Phaidon

Zatoka, Slav (2016) *A Tale of Two Cities*, 26 April: http://californiamodern.tumblr.com/

RESOURCES

California Preservation Foundation: **www.californiapreservation.org/**

Craig Krull Gallery: **www.craigkrullgallery.com/Shulman/**

Docomomo: **www.docomomo-us.org/**

Getty Research Institute: **www.getty.edu/research/**

Julius Shulman Institute: **http://jsi.architecture.woodbury.edu/**

Los Angeles Conservancy: Modern Committee (ModCom): **www.laconservancy.org/modcom**

National Register of Historic Places: **www.nps.gov/nr/index.htm**

Palm Springs Historical Society: **http://pshistoricalsociety.org/**

Palm Springs Modern Committee: **http://psmodcom.org/**

Palm Springs Modernism Week: **www.modernismweek.com/**

Palm Springs Preservation Foundation: **www.pspreservationfoundation.org/**

Society of Architectural Historians, Southern California Chapter: **www.sahscc.org/**

Visual Acoustics: The Modernism of Julius Shulman, A film by Eric Bricker: **www.juliusshulmanfilm.com/**

NOTES

[i] Melton (2009)

[ii] Walker (2009)

[iii] Goldberger (1989)

[iv] *TIME* (2016)

[v] Rattenbury (2002)

[vi] Kaufman (1969)

[vii] Rockwood (2007)

[viii] Sullivan (1924)

[ix] Loos (1908)

[x] Le Corbusier (1924)

[xi] Wright (1911)

[xii] Le Corbusier (1924)

[xiii] Hitchcock and Johnson (1932)

[xiv] Rikala de Noreiga (2010)

[xv] Ibid

[xvi] Ibid

[xvii] Ibid

[xviii] Ibid

[xix] Teicholz (2007)

[xx] Shulman and Harris (2000)

[xxi] Melton (2009)

[xxii] Rikala de Noreiga (2010)

[xxiii] Shulman (2000)

[xxiv] Ibid

[xxv] Nakano (2005)

[xxvi] Lamprecht (2000)

[xxvii] Calcagno and Nikolova (n.d.)

[xxviii] Le Corbusier (1924)

[xxix] Architecture critic P. Morton Shand (1934), quoted in Katzenstein (2008)

[xxx] Woods (2009)

[xxxi] Bayley (2014)

[xxxii] Campany (2014)

[xxxiii] Moholy-Nagy and Hoffmann (1932)

[xxxiv] Campany (2014)

[xxxv] Entry for 10 March 1924 in *The Daybooks of Edward Weston*, quoted in Newhall (1975)

[xxxvi] Moholy-Nagy (1922)

[xxxvii] MacCarthy (2006)

[xxxviii] Betjeman (1938)

[xxxix] Hitchcock (1936)

[xl] Shulman and Harris (2000)

[xli] Zatoka (2016)

[xlii] Crosse (2009)

[xliii] Kristal (2009)

[xliv] Jencks (2013)

[xlv] Bayley (2014)

[xlvi] Ciampaglia (2015)

[xlvii] Shulman (2000)

[xlviii] Ibid

[xlix] Cartier-Bresson (1952)

[l] Zatoka (2016)

[li] Kristal (2009)

[lii] Ibid

[liii] Ibid

[liv] Shulman and Harris (2000)

[lv] Rikala de Noreiga (2010)

[lvi] Quddus (2014)

[lvii] Icon Photography School (2011)

[lviii] Shulman and Harris (2000)

[lix] Ibid

[lx] Melton (2009)

[lxi] Spence (2015)

[lxii] Kristal (2009)

[lxiii] Ford (1946)

[lxiv] Shulman, Gössel and O'Gehry (1998)

[lxv] Rikala de Noreiga (2010)

[lxvi] Ibid

[lxvii] Smith and McCoy (1989)

[lxviii] Shulman and Serraino (2000)

[lxix] International Center of Photography (n.d.)

[lxx] Miles Gardiner (2005)

[lxxi] Ibid

[lxxii] Kaplan (2011)

[lxxiii] Shulman and Harris (2000)

[lxxiv] Kristal (2015)

[lxxv] Shulman and Harris (2000)

[lxxvi] Shulman (1977)

[lxxvii] Calcagno and Nikolova (2015)

[lxxviii] Kristal (2015)

[lxxix] *Visual Acoustics: The Modernism of Julius Shulman*

BLU-RAY SPECIAL FEATURES

A FILM FOR LIVING IN
Will Paice and Eric Bricker discuss Julius Shulman and the making of *Visual Acoustics*.
Produced and Directed by Eric Bricker, Will Paice and Omar McAlpine
© 2018 Network

PAICE ON SHULMAN
Will Paice examines Julius Shulman's style and legacy.
Directed and Edited by Omar McAlpine
© 2018 Network

DELETED SCENES
Nearly four minutes of deleted scenes from *Visual Acoustics*.

ORIGINAL TRAILER

ARCHIVE: LET'S RAP
In this archive edition of Los Angeles KTTV's discussion show, Julius Shulman debates the impact of economic growth on the environment and community with Gilbert W. Ferguson.

GALLERIES
Shulman: Origins and Icons
Shulman in Color

ARTHOUSE FILMS, CURIOUSLY BRIGHT ENTERTAINMENT and SHULMAN PROJECT PARTNERS, L.P. in association with OUT OF THE BOX PRODUCTIONS Present "VISUAL ACOUSTICS" Design and Animation TROLLBACK + COMPANY Composer CHARLIE CAMPAGNA Editor CHARLTON McMILLAN Directors of Photography AIKEN WEISS, DANTE SPINOTTI Co-Writers LISA HUGHES, JESSICA HUNDLEY Writers ERIC BRICKER, PHIL ETHINGTON Associate Producer ROSE NIELSEN Co-Producers WILL PAIGE, FREDERIC LIEBERT Production Consultant KAREN LEE ARBEENY Producers ERIC BRICKER, BABETTE ZILCH Executive Producers LISA HUGHES, MICHELLE OLIVER Narrator DUSTIN HOFFMAN Director ERIC BRICKER www.juliusshulmanfilm.com

	MAIN FEATURE	SPECIAL FEATURES
PICTURE	1080p HD 1.78:1	1080p HD 1.78:1
SOURCE	1080p HD 1.78:1	1080p HD 1.78:1
SOUND	5.1 / 2.0	Stereo
SUBTITLES	English	None
DURATION	84 minutes approx.	

networkonair.com

network

Packaging Design © 2019 Network
Distributed by Network Distributing
Limited under license from New Video
Group Inc., a Cinedigm Company.
Sleeve design by Rob White

7958101

Exempt from classification